Library of
Davidson College

Prayers

for

Public Worship

Prayers for Public Worship

by Carl T. Uehling

Philadelphia
Fortress Press

FOR JEAN

© 1972 by Fortress Press

All rights reserved. No part of this publication may be reproduced, stored in a retrieval system, or transmitted in any form or by any means, electronic, mechanical, photocopying, recording, or otherwise, without the prior permission of the copyright owner.

Library of Congress Catalog Card Number 72-75657

ISBN-0-8006-0234-X

1681C72   Printed in the U.S.A.   1-234

Contents

Preface		ix
I.	Prayers of General Purpose (1-20)	1
II.	Shorter Prayers of General Purpose (21-27)	45
III.	Prayers for the Church Year	55
	Advent (28)	56
	Christmas (29)	58
	Christmas (30)	60
	Lent (31)	63
	Lent (32)	65
	Palm Sunday (33)	67
	Holy Week (34)	69
	Holy Week (35)	71
	Easter (36)	73
	Easter (37)	74
	Pentecost (38)	76
	Thanksgiving (39)	78
	Last Sunday after Pentecost (40)	80
IV.	Prayers for the Secular Seasons	83
	New Year (41)	84
	Winter (42)	87

v

	Spring (43)	89
	Summer (44)	91
	Fall (45)	93
	College Education (46)	95
	National Elections (47)	97
	Christmas Preparation (48)	100
V.	Prayers Especially for Use when Communion is Offered (49-54)	103
VI.	Prayers for Other Purposes	115
	Family (55)	116
	A Time of Tragedy and Shock (56)	118
	A Time of Great Joy (57)	120
	Peace (58)	122
VII.	A Set of Affirmations and Petitions for Use in Ecumenical Gatherings	125
VIII.	Intercessions	133
	For the People of God	134
	For Evangelism	134
	For the Ministry	134
	For Seminaries	134
	For Church Meetings	135
	For World Missions	135

For the Persecuted	135
For Dialogue	136
For the Sick	136
For the Seriously Injured	136
For the Dying	136
For the Sorrowing	137
For the New Year	137
For the Fruits of the Earth in Their Season	137
For Elections	138
For the Nation	138
For Our Leaders	138
For Those in the Armed Forces	138
For Social Justice	139
For the Community	139
For Brotherhood	139
For Peace	140
For the Poor	140
For the Imprisoned	140
For the Aged	141
For Industrial Peace	141
For the Unemployed	141
For Contending with the Perils of Abundance	142
For Those Who Travel	142

	For Students	142
	For Those About to be Married	142
	For the Children	143
	For a Wedding Anniversary	143
	For Family Life	143
	For Christians and Jews	144
	For Those Who Have Just Been Baptized	144
	For Those Who Have Just Been Married	144
	For the Memory of the Dead in Christ	145
IX.	Dialogue Prayers	147
	Vocations (59)	148
	Youth (60)	152
	Various Ages (61)	154
	Men and Women (62)	157
	Various Congregational Concerns (63)	160

Preface

Sometimes called the "pastoral prayer," or the "general prayer," or the "prayer of the church," or more recently, the "intercessions," prayers that seek to be broadly inclusive of the varied concerns of the people have long been a part of the worship of the Christian church. As traditions happened to dictate, such prayers took the form of extemporaneous and often homiletical addresses, or they were more carefully crafted statements prepared prior to the service, or they were repeated, Sunday after Sunday, because they had semiofficial status through their placement in service books.

Each such form had its virtue. The extemporaneous prayer, with its direct relation to the emotional level of the congregation and its reflection of the pastor's ability to touch deeply upon the sensitivities of his people, could have the effect of deepening personal commitment and strengthening faith. The prayer prepared in advance by the minister could weave together the various ingredients of the morning's worship—hymns, lessons, sermon—and offer a satisfying conclusion to the concerns of the day. The prayer of the service book continued that volume's literary quality, and provided, as well, an overview of the proper concerns of the church.

But there were failings, too, some more obvious than others. Extemporaneous prayers could be wordy, and embarrassingly deficient in grammar and theology. Prayers assembled by a single person, regardless of his training or his competence, tended to be repetitious in emphasizing that person's own special interests. And the prayer of the service book became dry and formal, particularly if used regularly.

There were two other failings of our typical prayers, however, to which this collection seeks to address itself.

Our prayers have been in the language of our liturgies, a rich and unique jargon which continues worthy of esthetic appreciation, but which is not appropriate to the experience of the people of God in the world of today. This "holy talk" included not only the quaint forms of address dating back to Elizabethan England, but also words and phrases which could not be easily comprehended in terms of contemporary life situations.

The prayers in this volume are in contemporary language, and every effort has been made to render them easily understood. The literary expression remains, however, chaste and subdued, in the conviction that they will thus be most appropriate to the greatest number of people. The efforts of various clergymen to render liturgical material into even more popular idioms is to be admired, but the intention of this present work is to create a collection of prayers that can be used helpfully in any form of worship, and which does not call attention to itself by the extremity of its phrases.

Another failing, typically, has been that our prayers have been the prayers of our clergymen, and not of our people. They have continued, therefore, the ancient superstition which holds that only the ordained can address God properly or efficaciously. That superstition is beginning to be broken, and we are coming to see that what happens when a Christian people gather is most properly determined by those people, and this book is intended to be a contribution to that process.

Most of these prayers can be read by one person, by the minister of the church at his accustomed time and in his accustomed station. But most of them, as well, can be read by more than one person, and often by several voices, or by an entire congregation. The various type faces and paragraph arrangements are intended to suggest this kind of use by many different people.

That use, again, can occur because of the arbitrary action of the clergyman as the "designer" of a congregation's worship. But it also could occur because small groups of people gather for the purpose of planning the congregation's worship, week by week, discussing the pressing concerns of the community and the plans of the pastor relative to his teaching and preaching, then assembling the ingredients for the service forthcoming.

This book can be used in a number of different ways as a part of the worship of the people of God. A given prayer can be selected, and various paragraphs assigned to different members of the congregation, to be read by them from their places. Or, the entire text of a prayer can be duplicated and placed in the hands of the people, with sections designated to be read by the whole congregation. Sections can be deleted, or inserted from other prayers in this book or from still other sources.

The material in this book, of course, is copyrighted, and it is illegal to reproduce it in any form under normal circumstances. However, permission is hereby granted for the reproduction in whole or in part of materials from this book for the purpose of public worship, provided such use does not constitute a means to avoid the purchase of this book.

Most of the prayers include an obvious space which indicates a likely place for the insertion of a petition of local concern. This would most often be for the sick, or for the giving of special thanks, or for some other pressing issue. Depending upon the nature of that local concern another place in the prayer might be more appropriate.

A number of friends have read portions of this manuscript, and have offered helpful suggestions, for which I am grateful. They include Eugene L. Brand, Robert M. Brusic, Gilbert E. Doan, David R. Gerberding, Edward T. Horn, III, Karl E. Kniseley, Ralph W. Loew, Paul H. A. Noren, Arthur L. Ruths, James M. Singer, Robert W. Stackel, and Ralph R. Van Loon.

CARL T. UEHLING

Philadelphia, Pennsylvania
Pentecost, 1972

I

Prayers of General Purpose

Eternal Lord,
you have always existed,
and still you are the creator of time and space.
You live and move within all times and all spaces,
and beyond all time and space.
You have made us to be your own,
and given us our very life and being.
We honor you as our God,
and we give to you our love
as children to a father.
> *We see that love most clearly in Jesus Christ,*
> *and pray that by the work of your Spirit in us*
> *we may have the grace and wisdom to follow him.*
> *May it happen that even as your favor rests upon us*
> *in designating us to be your servants,*
> *we now become the means of healing and help*
> *in this world,*
> *the means of service and peace,*
> *the means of justice and truth.*

As there are many with special needs,
look to their needs
and stir the hearts of men with the compassion to serve.

> *Cause all useful arts and worthy labors to flourish,*
> *and give guidance, especially,*
> *to those who take into their hands*
> *the lives of others:*

doctors and nurses;
pilots, engineers, and drivers;
managers and mechanics;
teachers, pastors, and social workers;
legislators, policemen, and firemen;
service men and women;
secretaries and salesmen;
housewives and farmers;
and all others upon whom we must depend.

Look to us in our need for peace.
Stifle the pride that grips us
while men still die in fruitless battles.
Renew the church,
and give the gospel those new forms
and clearer understanding
that will make plain its challenge in the world emerging.

For our fellowship as your people,
O God,
we are thankful.
Help us to affirm our oneness
by our common service to each other
and to the world.
Go with us on the journeys of life,
and bring us at the last to our eternal home,
through Jesus Christ, our Lord,
who lives and rules with you and the Spirit,
one God forever. Amen.

2

Eternal God, our father,
we know that it is as if we are held
in the hollow of your hand.
Our life and our times are in your keeping.
The flight of a sparrow
and the destiny of a man
are both within your concern.
You are the source of all that exists,
the power beyond all powers,
and still you come to us in love.
How beyond our understanding
that you should care about this small planet,
know us by name,
and give us your son.
Grant us the grace, O God, to comprehend this gift,
that we may give evidence of our gratitude
by lives of sacrifice and service.
> *As with the compassion of Jesus Christ,*
> *father,*
> *look upon our needs.*
> *Enable the sick and the infirm to receive the healing*
> *that is your intention for their lives,*
> *and strength of spirit*
> *sufficient for the adversity they face.*
> *Comfort the bereaved,*
> *counsel the confused,*
> *and look not in judgment but in pity*

*upon those who in this age of human achievement
have lost their faith.*

Consider our continuing needs
for sustenance
and education
and purpose.
Instill within us the desire to help others
without destroying their hope to help themselves.
Undergird the church with new power.
Defend her from those aggressive outsiders
who would rejoice over her death
as well as from indifferent insiders
who would kill her more surely by ignoring her.
> *Calm the nervousness of our world*
> *by giving sense to our rulers.*
> *Be the guide of the president of this nation,*
> *the governor of this state,*
> *and all others who have the responsibility of authority.*

Preserve within us a lively hope,
O father,
that throughout this earthly journey
we may be confident of the coming of your kingdom
here among us,
as well as of the eternal home promised by your son,
our savior Jesus Christ,
who lives with you and the Spirit,
one God forever. Amen.

3

Our God and father,
through the tumult of this world
you are always able to come to us with your peace.
In the midst of every adversity
you offer to us your strength.
In our most hopeless hour
you point us to a time when all will be well
because we will be with you.
We believe in you, O Lord,
and we are grateful for every evidence of your love.
Help us in our unbelief,
lest in foolish despair
we fall away from you.
> *Father,*
> *our human nature is very much with us.*
> *We are oppressed by the knowledge of our failings.*
> *Come with your power and health*
> *to the great multitude of our misfortunes,*
>> *that those who in poverty*
>> *struggle to stay alive*
>> *may be given your assistance;*
>> *that those who are the victims*
>> *of infirmity and illness*
>> *may have relief from pain,*
>> *new measures of strength,*
>> *and the will to endure;*
>> *that those who live under the shadow*

*of difficult relationships
may have patience and understanding.*

Touch with your love those places in our world
where needs are so apparent,
but prevent us from thinking
that we are not also in need.
Give your church the vision to risk great things
for your kingdom and your people.
Guide the leaders of men in every place,
kings and prime ministers and presidents,
governors and mayors and magistrates.
Remember your church and your people,
bishops and presidents, pastors and priests,
all who in their way would serve
your kingdom and your son.
*Help us, O God,
to see more clearly the extent of your gift to us
in Jesus Christ.
Spur us to gratitude,
that we may care more for him and his concerns
than we do for the host of other things
that clamor for our attention.
May he abide and rule in our hearts,
our Lord and savior,
one God with you and the Spirit forever. Amen.*

4

Our father God,
you lavish all the goodness of this world upon us
for our use and our delight,
you intend for us purposes beyond both imagination
and achievement,
and though we have turned away from your love,
you have sent to us a savior.
We give you our praise,
the worship of our hearts and the service of our lives,
our wonder at your greatness and our commitment to you.
> *Because we know of your desire,*
> *father,*
> *that our earth be fair and all men be one,*
> *we pray for your continuing concern,*
> *that it may touch all manner and conditions of men.*
> *Work by your Spirit*
> *so that the conflicts which threaten to engulf the world*
> *may be averted,*
> *and those tensions*
> *eating with their acids into men and nations*
> *may be forgotten.*

Guide the president of our nation,
the governor of our state,
the mayors of our cities,
and all leaders everywhere that they may seek your will.
Cause the many ways of injustice to be lessened,
especially in this land where all men ought to be free.

Give freedom, O God,
and in the giving of it
teach also responsibility and understanding
to all who now dispute with each other,
lest a greater slavery engulf us.
Look in pity upon any who suffer
because of our human weakness,
and give opportunity to the poor,
healing to the sick,
hope to the dying,
and comfort to the bereaved.

O Lord,
be with those who look upon the days ahead
and find them grey and empty.
May they yet believe,
and in believing have courage and strength and peace.
> *Walk with us now,*
> *father,*
> *as we return to our responsibilities within the world.*
> *Even as you care for the unfortunate,*
> *help us to care.*
> *Even as you invite us to the work of your kingdom,*
> *cause us to answer with joy and devotion,*
> *through Christ, our Lord,*
> *who lives and rules with you and the Spirit,*
> *one God forever. Amen.*

5

O father,
our lives are your invention.
Our times are in your hands.
In love you gave us birth.
In love you came in Jesus Christ,
that all of eternity may be opened to us,
and that we may learn to live for you
without fear and in freedom.
We thank you for your love,
and pray for the undergirding of your Spirit
so that we may increasingly give ourselves to you.

> *Many of your children are unable to see you in their lives*
> *and conclude that you are gone.*
> *Help us to see you everywhere,*
> *by the clear evidence of your love.*
> *Reach through the willing hands of your people*
> *to the needs of men.*
> *Comfort those who are in distress or sorrow.*
> *Ease the pain of those who face the end of life.*
> *Feed those who are hungry,*
> *clothe those who are naked,*
> *house those who are homeless,*
> *and correct the inequities of our world*
> *that cause some to have enough to waste*
> *and others not enough to live.*

Be the God of all nations,
and cause honest governments and conscientious rulers
to prosper.
Bless by your Spirit
the leaders of our community,
the governor of the state,
the president of our country.
Be the companion of our service men and women
as they discharge their duties,
and hasten the day when spears shall be turned into plows,
when men shall no longer bear arms against one another.

Prosper, O God,
the arts and industry,
schools and churches,
communities and homes.
Stop us from frantically serving ourselves,
and restore a sense of commitment
to one another,
and the wisdom to walk in the ways of peace.
Give substance to our best hopes,
and courage to dream noble dreams,
that in the light come to earth
by your love in Jesus Christ
we may yet build his kingdom,
through the same Jesus Christ, your son, our Lord,
who lives and rules with you and the Spirit,
one God forever. Amen.

6

Our father God,
we dare to come before you not as we ought to be but as we are,
in love with ourselves,
confident to the point of arrogance,
doubting you and your existence
even as we address ourselves to you.
But such are the fashions of our age,
and for them, as they are found in us,
we ask your patience and forgiveness.

> *You are the creator of our world and of each one of us,*
> *our redeemer,*
> *our comforter,*
> *unchanged from the testimony of men in times past,*
> *competent to meet our most complex need,*
> *concerned for us through our every path in life.*
> *Now when men make their own miracles*
> *and presume their own divinity,*
> *graciously help us to believe,*
> *with fervor and with hope.*

And, O God,
as men lose hope in this world where evil spawns evil
and virtues disappear,
come in your love and give us your help.
Work through all men everywhere,
even those we call our enemies,
for the building of peace.
Silence the guns, and establish justice.

*Direct those who have competence and insight
to attempt to solve the problems
that plague our race and our nation:*
- *the soaring population of the earth;*
- *the lessening of our resources;*
- *the poisoning of our environment;*

*and reach with compassion to those first victims
of this abuse of our heritage,
the poor and the disadvantaged.*

Multiply the good works of men to men,
and prosper our efforts to heal,
to make right, to build.
Give us so strong a sense of your presence
that we will be able to tolerate confusion,
accept change,
and live with the rush that is all around us,
committed to you
and so committed to living creatively
for one another.

*By the achievements of men,
we could think ourselves to be gods
walking the face of the earth.
Save us from such conceit,
and make us instead to be persons
of sacrifice and concern,
through Jesus Christ, your son, our Lord,
who lives and rules with you and the Spirit,
one God forever. Amen.*

7

Father,
look upon your people,
and reach out to us according to our need for you.
We believe that you will answer our needs,
dear Lord,
that you are concerned about us.
Even though you are the master of all of the universe
and we are as dust,
still we have the assurance of your love,
and we are grateful.
> *We find ourselves,*
> *O God,*
> *in pleasant ways,*
> *and we thank you for this land promising*
> *freedom and opportunity,*
> *rich with fruits and resources,*
> *wherein we may worship you*
> *without fear.*
> *Yet there are those in this world*
> *and in this nation*
> *who are oppressed and stricken by adversity.*
> *We pray for them,*
> *that their needs, of whatever dimensions,*
> *may be met.*

Reach to the poor,
and to those saddened by tragedy.
Restore liberty to the enslaved.

Convert those who would pass judgment upon others
because of race or creed or nationality.
According to your mercy and will, give new health to the sick,
and courage to the dying.

*Cause this congregation to grow
in the numbers of those committed to serve you
even above the service of themselves.
Work with your Spirit throughout all of the church,
that the darkness of this present age
may be dispelled by the light of your gospel.
Help the rulers of our world to seek peace
and pursue it.*
O God,
part the shadows that so often perplex us,
not that we may come to a knowledge of all things,
but that even without perfect understanding
we may see the light of Jesus Christ
as sufficient for our lives and our world,
who lives and rules with you and the Spirit,
one God forever. Amen.

8

O Lord, our God,
only you are eternal,
and it is only to you that we can turn when everything else fails.
All of our human wonders are as castles in the sand
when compared to you.
We praise you for your power
as it has worked for our good,
for your grace reaching new to us each day,
for your love expressed in Jesus Christ, our savior.
> *Look upon us,*
> *O Lord,*
> *in our conceits and in our distresses.*
> *Cause us to become more constant in our devotion,*
> *more fervent in our prayers,*
> *more determined to walk in the steps of your son.*

To that intent,
dear God,
point us to the needs that cry
for our presence, our hands, and our money.
Make us so disturbed at the thought of poverty and injustice
that we will strain our resources for the help of others.
Reach in pity to those for whom life has lost its taste,
and give new hope to the bereaved,
new courage to the endangered,
new assurance to the anxious,
new trust and confidence
to those who find the road covered with the unknown.

Father,
look upon the unsettled nature of our world,
and give your peace.
Guide all who endeavor to lead the people,
and endow them with the patience
to understand the problems
of minorities and enemies and the weak.
Prosper the efforts of those who counsel together
for the purpose of bringing peace to all men,
and frustrate the designs of those who live by the sword.
Cause your church in every place
to declare your truth with conviction and perception,
that men may come to believe in you
and work for the building of your kingdom.
Be with and among your people,
that in this place we may be found faithful
to your word.
As we are strangers and pilgrims,
Lord,
go with us upon every path and to every place,
that assured of your presence
we may live more fully for the loving service
of one another,
like him whom we acknowledge as our savior,
even Jesus Christ, your son,
who lives and rules with you and the Spirit,
one God forever. Amen.

9

God, our father:
we belong to you.
We are your children because we have been reborn of your love.
We are your people because we have been gathered in your son.
For what we are,
and for all that you have done for our good,
we give you our thanks.
> *For life and for the abundance of this earth,*
> *for richness of field and orchard, mine and well,*
> *for industry and commerce in bountiful production,*
> *and for all our treasured things,*

we give you our thanks.
> *For the opportunities of life,*
> *for schools and cultures,*
> *for the skills of our science*
> *and the imagination of our technology,*
> *for the talents of artists,*
> *and for the labors of all honest men,*

we give you our thanks.
> *For the compassions of life,*
> *for the healers of mind and body,*
> *for the brave who seek to right the wrongs of our society,*
> *for social workers, lawyers, and housewives,*
> *for managers, truck drivers, and teachers,*
> *for machinists, bankers, and merchants,*
> *for musicians, clerks, and secretaries,*
> *for all who in their way would give life grace,*

we give you our thanks.
> *Look upon us in our need.*
> *Reach to us with your continuing concern.*
> *Uphold us and renew us.*

Frustrate our designs when they are corrupt
with our self-conceits.
Make us stumble under the weight of our self-concerns.
Stifle in our throats the sound of our self-pity.
> *And empower us to rise to the needs around us.*

As there are those within our reach
and in our world
who are discouraged and lonely,
afflicted and diseased,
sorrowing and disturbed,
> *move within us to move to them,*
> *to love them and help them,*
> *to give them assurance of your love.*

As peace and the pursuit of peace are scorned by the worldly
and the object of their wrath,
as war and the threat of war
is increasingly the blood of our economy,
as wise men elect silence and good men bow to fear,
> *move within us to seek the truth and to speak it,*
> *to work for peace and justice for all men,*
> *to build your kingdom.*

As our institutions stand threatened
by the changes of our day,
as our government and schools,
our families and churches,
all struggle for the new stance a new world demands,

as our leaders are also lost and perplexed,
> *move within us to bring strength and purpose,*
> *to encourage the right and correct the wrong,*
> *to find those new means which will best serve us*
> *and those who follow us.*

Keep us faithful to your trust in us,
and to your people,
that though we meet with reversal and failure,
we may yet know the power you give
so that men may fulfill your will.
> *Help us, O God, to serve you by serving others,*
> *through Jesus Christ, your son, our Lord,*
> *who lives and rules with you and the Spirit,*
> *one God forever. Amen.*

10

Eternal God, our father,
we are your children, formed of your love.
We are your people, called to your service.
>*For the gift of life,*
>*and for the riches we have from you,*

we give you our thanks.
>*For your concern reaching to our lives,*
>*made clear in the life of Jesus Christ,*
>*who lived for others,*

we give you our thanks.
>*For the many continuing ways of your love,*
>*for the gathered community of the faithful,*
>*and for the hope you give*
>*for the coming of your kingdom,*

we give you our thanks.
>*Look in pity upon all in need.*
>>*Uphold any who are discouraged*
>>*by the difficulties of life.*
>>*Strengthen the sick.*
>>*Comfort those in sorrow.*
>>*Guide the bewildered and confused.*

Grant us the grace to see the full measure
of our own responsibility for the relief of suffering.
Enable us to reach helpfully to the poor,
the homeless, the forgotten, the alone.

> *Grant an end to oppression,*
> *a resolution to the conditions*
> *by which some have much*
> *and many have nothing,*
> *a new climate of freedom and opportunity*
> *for all people everywhere.*
> *That all these things may come to be,*
> *help us, good Lord.*

Direct us in all our ways.
Help our institutions to develop
the new structures a new age demands.
To that end let your Spirit work
within our schools and our churches and our governments.

> *Bless all who bear responsibility for others,*
> *and give them a sense of your purpose in what they do:*
> *businessmen and teachers, pastors and scientists.*

Transportation workers and entertainers,
housewives and secretaries,
doctors and nurses,
journalists and mechanics,
and all in useful occupations in all places.

> *And that we may all know our lives*
> *and our work to be within your concern,*
> *help us, good Lord.*
> *Guide us in the ways of peace.*

Counsel our officials in their difficult tasks.
Where our government acts in accordance with your will,
prosper those actions;
and where it acts contrary to your will,
correct it.

*Be the companion of those
who serve our nation in the armed forces,
or through alternate service as conscientious objectors,
or by the giving of themselves
in underdeveloped nations
or among the disadvantaged in our country.
Give the assurance of your love
to those who suffer greatly because of war,
the wounded and the dying,
the homeless and the distressed.*
Bless our enemies, and let truth and justice prevail.
*Give us peace, O God.
Give us peace.*
Help us, good Lord,
through Jesus Christ, your son and our savior,
who lives and rules with you and the Spirit,
one God forever. Amen.

11

Lord God eternal,
we turn to you in thanksgiving and praise,
for you are the source of our lives
and we know that we belong to you.
For all that we have and all that we are because of your love,
we offer our gratitude.
> *For food and drink,*
> *for clothing and shelter,*
> *for friends and families,*
> *for all who serve us*
> *by their professions and their concern,*
> *for pleasant days and the beauties of this earth,*
> *for books and scholars,*
> *for science and learning,*
> *and for the marvels of our modern age,*
> *for music and laughter, poetry and color,*
> *for help in times of need,*
> *for strength for moments of weakness,*

for all that we have and all that we are because of your love,
we offer our gratitude.
> *We give you our thanks.*
> *Yet keep us aware,*
> *O God,*
> *of those who do not share our wealth,*
> *whose lot is harsh and whose means are few,*
> *who struggle with life and often fail.*

Look upon the poor of the earth,
the handicapped, and the oppressed,
and reach to them with your love.
> *Help us to help them.*
> *Guide us into paths of useful service,*
> *and give us the will to serve*
> *in every place of need.*
> *Nor let us forget our responsibility*
> *to the whole body of our humanity.*
> *Give us a sense of belonging to one another,*
> *despite our nationalities,*
> *our races, and our religions.*

Uphold those who are set in positions of authority,
and give them the grace to be wise, kind, and just,
charitable and seekers after peace.
> *Let your peace come to our earth,*
> *dear father.*
> *Bring peace forever.*
> *Cause men and nations to live in justice and harmony,*
> *with freedom for all.*
> *Go with us as we go from here,*
> *that in all our ways*
> *we may be confident of your presence.*

When we are discouraged,
give us a new heart and a new spirit.
When we are tired,
help us to find new strength.
When we are afraid,
renew our awareness of your power
and purpose for our lives.

So may we serve you,
O God,
by being your people,
in service to all who need us,
and happy for your love;
through Jesus Christ, your son, our Lord,
who lives and rules with you and the Spirit,
one God forever. Amen.

12

Eternal father,
we dare to come to you
not because we are in any way worthy of your attention,
but only because you have taught us
to turn to you in prayer and supplication.
You have loved us beyond all telling.
We thank you for all we have from you,
for the very breath of life,
for food and shelter,
for the comforts that you give to us,
and for your mercy in Jesus Christ, our savior.
> *Help us that we may continue to know him as our Lord.*
> *Guide us*
> *that despite the pressures of the lives we lead*
> *we may still turn to him*
> *in every time of need.*
> *Preserve us*
> *from seeking any other answer than him*
> *to our despair or emptiness,*
> *our weakness or anxiety.*

Let the light of Christ shed light
in all the dark places of our world,
dear God.
Give to those who are in any kind of need
the things that they require:
food and clothing,
shelter and medicine,

relief from oppression,
trust in your mercy and assurance of your love.
> *Cause truth and righteousness*
> *to prevail in our land and in all places.*
> *Give understanding to our leaders,*
> *the governor of this state*
> *and the president of this nation.*
> *Uphold your church with your power,*
> *and cause her institutions and congregations*
> *to fulfill your purpose*
> *in the service of others.*

Walk with us, we pray, upon every path in life.
Protect those who journey far from home,
be the companion of our loved ones wherever they may be,
give the sick such healing as may be your will,
and pour peace and understanding into the hearts of the bereaved.

> *Help us, each one,*
> *that we may find in the wilderness of our lives*
> *him who alone is our Lord,*
> *even Jesus Christ, your son, our savior,*
> *who lives and rules with you and the Spirit,*
> *one God forever. Amen.*

13

O Lord, our God and father,
your goodness is beyond our telling.
Your love is greater by far than our deserving.
For all of your gifts,
for grace and mercy without end,
we give you our thanks and our praise.
> *Look, we pray, upon all in need.*
> *Strengthen the weak,*
> *encourage the faltering,*
> *restore the faith of those who doubt.*

Direct us to the hungry,
the naked, and the homeless,
lest in our abundance we fail to be good stewards
of what you have given to us.
As any of our loved ones are ill, or in sorrow,
give them whatever may best serve them in their trouble,
and your peace.

> *Reach with your power to all of the world,*
> *drunk as it is with shallow concerns*
> *for grandeur and petty human achievement.*
> *Where men are engaged in acts of violence or war,*
> *cause sanity to be restored.*
> *Silence the angry instruments of death.*
> *Be with service men and women everywhere,*
> *and hasten the day when they may return*
> *to their homes and families.*

Be the Lord of all who have the responsibility of authority,
especially the governor of this state
and the president of this nation.
Help them to discharge their duties with wisdom
and concern for the common good.
> *Bless all useful occupations,*
> *come with your love into the homes of our land,*
> *give guidance to the young,*
> *endow with new and sacred purpose*
> *all institutions of mercy and education,*
> *and give us direction*
> *that we may find the means of useful service*
> *within our communities and among all people.*

Keep us honest,
dear God,
to ourselves.
So may we avoid pretense and sham and hypocrisy.
So may we be content to be your own,
under the lordship of your son and our savior, Jesus Christ,
who lives and rules with you and the Spirit,
one God forever. Amen.

14

Lord God, our father,
by whom we are formed and sustained,
in whom we have life and reason for living,
we thank you for your love,
> *for the mercy undeserved*
> *that goes before and follows after us,*
> *for your son, our savior Jesus Christ.*
> *Cause us so to cherish him in our hearts*
> *that the attractions of this world may not prevail,*
> *that he shall be our Lord*
> *even as other responsibilities*
> *also exercise their measure of dominion,*
> *that all of life, for us,*
> *may be his growing kingdom.*

Father,
we know of your concern for any who are in need,
but we pray for them
that we may be at one with you in love.
> *Look in pity upon the sick*
> *the anguished,*
> *the bewildered,*
> *the sorrowing.*
>> *Give new hope to those who cannot see light,*
>> *who cannot look with confidence to their future.*
> *Cause many arms of mercy*
> *to reach to the many in our world*
> *without adequate food and shelter.*

*Rule the heads of the nations,
and give counsel to the leaders of our country,
that in these days of stress at home and abroad
they may clearly see the course of action
best for the people.*
*Grant peace in our world,
with freedom for your people and abundance.
Help your church,
her congregations and her agencies,
that the challenges of the moment
may be met with faith and competence.*

And show us the sense,
dear God,
to keep a balance
between the doing of good for others
and the devotion we owe to you,
that we may come closer
to the example of him who went about doing good
even as he proclaimed the gospel,
your son, our savior Jesus Christ,
who lives and rules with you and the Spirit,
one God forever. Amen.

15

Gracious father,
you have made all of us your children,
formed us by your design and destined us for your purposes,
for which we praise you as our creator
and acknowledge you as our Lord.
> *You have given us assurance of your love,*
> *coming to this world in Jesus Christ*
> *so that we may know you.*
> *As by his example*
> *we do know the dimensions of your concern,*
> *we are bold to pray,*
> *not as if to awaken you to your work,*
> *but rather that we may ourselves be guided*
> *to the doing of it.*

Therefore, O God,
feed the poor,
> *and help us to share our affluence.*

O God,
heal the sick,
> *and help us to reach with compassion*
> *to any who are afflicted.*

O God,
cause justice and truth to prevail,
> *and help us to be brave enough*
> *to live justly with our neighbors.*

O God,
prosper your church,

> *and help us rightly to understand*
> *your will for this, the body of Christ on earth,*
> *and then to do it.*

O God,
counsel our rulers,
> *and help us so to participate*
> *in the democratic process*
> *that we will be governed by those who represent us*
> *and not by tyrants.*

O God,
bring peace on earth,
> *and help us to overcome our silence and our fear*
> *so that by the expressed will of your people*
> *wars will stop.*

We live in tumultuous times,
dear father,
and our heads swim with the pressure of what happens
even as our hearts are heavy
because of the character of what happens.
Come to us in our distress with your strength.
Give us new assurance of your love,
and new confidence in your eternal purpose.
> *So may it be*
> *that as our weakness is overcome by your power*
> *we may have the joy of those who view the morning,*
> *through Jesus Christ, your son, our Lord,*
> *who lives and rules with you and the Spirit,*
> *one God forever. Amen.*

16

O God, our father,
we are grateful to be your people,
to have been formed by your love,
to be the objects of your concern.
Continue to be our God and our father, we pray,
through all the changes of this present world,
that your kingdom may come,
and your will may be done.
> *Save us from ourselves, O Lord,*
> *from self-pity and self-love and self-serving.*
> *So may it be*
> *that we come to a new measure*
> *of pity and love and service to others.*

Enable us to be ministers of your grace
to the poor and the oppressed and the lost.
Guide us, that we may be wise
as we endeavor to fulfill our responsibilities
to other people,
both to our countrymen
as well as to those who live in distant lands.
> *Make clear the ways*
> *by which in our time*
> *inequities may be overcome*
> *and all men may live in freedom,*
> *with full opportunities for growth and happiness.*
> *As men anywhere are in need,*
> *be the source of their help.*

Look in pity upon the ill,
the discouraged,
the sorrowing.
Lighten their heavy moments,
give them new reasons for joy,
help them to endure and overcome.

> *Consider the institutions of men,*
> *give them power to break loose*
> *from the strictures of the past*
> *and adjust to our new age.*
> *Work within our schools*
> *and our churches and our homes,*
> *and enter upon the processes of our commerce*
> *and our science and our industry.*

Guide all rulers everywhere,
that they may seek the good of all people everywhere,
and that through their efforts
our world may be returned to peace.
Be with those who must yet enter upon any fields of battle.
Be the refuge of the dying
and the comfort of the wounded.
Bless our enemies and bring peace,
dear God,
bring peace.

> *These things we ask in the name of Jesus Christ,*
> *your son, our savior,*
> *who lives and rules with you and the Spirit,*
> *one God forever. Amen.*

17

Eternal Lord,
our savior Jesus Christ,
you came to this earth that we may come,
at the last,
to your home.
> *You taught us about life*
> *so that we may not fear death.*
> *You died so that we may live,*
> *and we believe you are God,*
> *knowing you overcame even death.*

For your victory and our hope,
we give you our praise.
> *Appear, we pray,*
> *in all the places of our lives.*
> *Turn us from empty motion*
> *to new purpose and meaning.*
> *Cover our confusions with your truth,*
> *that by your grace*
> *we may move with confidence upon all our ways.*
> *And for those times when all is wrong*
> *and we cannot see beyond the veil,*
> *give us patience with ourselves and others,*
> *mercy for all,*
> *and your peace.*

O God, our father,
by whose hand we were formed from the dust of the earth,
look upon your children,

and come to them with your love.
> *Cause the hungry to be fed,*
> *the naked to be clothed,*
> *the homeless to be housed.*
> *Reach to all who are in affliction,*
> *that they may have endurance and hope.*
> *Give understanding to those in sorrow.*
> *Cause us to be instruments*
> *of your creative will,*
> *and so may your kingdom be built.*

Holy Spirit,
counselor and guide,
be the continuing creator of the church,
giving new life
and the insight to reach with meaning
to the world as it is today.
> *Uphold your ministers*
> *as they labor with your people,*
> *and help all who believe*
> *to know themselves to be the priestly servants*
> *of Christ.*
> *Calm the angry hearts*
> *that would incite our world to conflict,*
> *and bless by your love*
> *the useful occupations of men.*

And to you, one God,
father, son, and Spirit,
who is, who was, and who will be, forever and ever,
be all praise and all glory. Amen.

18

Father,
we give you praise
for your love bestowed upon us,
love evident in our creation
and in the maintenance of our lives,
love made manifest in Jesus Christ,
who lived and died for us,
loving continuing through your Spirit
as you reach to us without ceasing
in order that we may be encouraged to live
in righteousness and peace.
> *Forgive us,*
> *O God,*
> *in that our ways have instead been too often*
> *the ways of war,*
> *in that we have neglected charity*
> *and exercised hasty judgments*
> *and thought first of ourselves.*
> *Direct us,*
> *that our doings may increasingly reflect*
> *your will.*

So much within our human condition
is in need of your love,
dear Lord.
Look in pity upon those who suffer in any way,
the sick and the poor and the confused,
the weak and the oppressed and the discouraged.

Where there is injustice in our land
let men arise whose passion is for freedom.
Where vested interests
suppress by their power
the expressions of others
let Davids come forth with the smooth stones of truth.

Cause those with grave responsibilities
to be faithful to the hopes of the people.
Accordingly give guidance to our mayor,
to the governor of this state,
to the president of this nation,
and to all rulers everywhere.
Forgive us
in that we have yet to bring forth
a more satisfactory answer
to the issues that divide the nations.
And as men are now engaged with their enemies
in conflict or war,
O God,
do not heed their pleas for victory,
but grant, instead, peace with justice and freedom for all.
Go with us now into the rest of this day,
and into whatever may be the circumstances of our lives,
that we may act with purpose
and to the doing of good for your people,
through Jesus Christ, your son, our Lord,
who lives and rules with you and the Spirit,
one God forever. Amen.

19

Eternal God,
whom we are privileged to know as our father,
for the love in which we came to life,
> *we give you our thanks.*

For the goodness you give to us new each day,
> *we give you our thanks.*

For the hope in which we live because of Jesus Christ,
> *we give you our thanks.*

Guide us when we turn from you,
restore us when our courage fails,
and keep us, though the world be dark,
close to your light and your truth.
> *We beg you to help us, good Lord.*

Our needs for your help are many and various.
Though our knowledge grows great,
ancient ills remain unsolved,
and your children die daily
because of poverty and ignorance and disease and war.
Work through us and through men everywhere,
that we may come to new levels
of sacrifice and compassion
and forgiveness and peace.
> *We beg you to help us, good Lord.*

Where your people are enslaved
because of the prejudice of others
or the misfortune of their circumstances,
break their chains and set them free.

Where responsibilities have been twisted
into opportunities for selfish gain,
come with judgment and correction.
Where the shallow sight of the centuries
blinds us to our brother's need,
strike away the shades
and open our hearts.
> *We beg you to help us, good Lord.*

Be with all in authority,
both here and in distant lands.
Guide with wisdom, and endue with concern
the mayor of this city,
the governor of this state,
the president of this nation.
Give help to your church as she attempts to know your will,
and protect her from the whitewashed tombs
that would destroy her in your name.
> *We beg you to help us, good Lord.*

Give us, in these days,
O God,
not rest but disquiet,
not satisfaction but turmoil,
not the path of ease
but that of the struggle to do the will of Christ,
our Lord and savior,
who lives and rules with you and the Spirit,
one God forever. Amen.

20

Our God and father,
we have so often set you in a framework of antiquity,
that your will has been of distant or historical interest,
your love a matter of record,
but not alive in our lives.
> *Forgive us*
> *for covering you with the dust of the ages*
> *so that we can live as if you do not live.*
> *Burst back into our lives with your truth,*
> *and cause us*
> *so to perceive your love for us in Christ*
> *that we can sense something of the pain*
> *of his cross*
> *and feel the compassion*
> *with which he dealt with men.*
> *Cause us to dedicate ourselves anew,*
> *to righteousness and service,*
> *to be those in this world of today*
> *who are willing to live for others*
> *even to the point of death.*

You know the power of your love.
Give us the confidence to believe
that you can overcome cruelty,
ignorance,
poverty,
injustice,
and all the evils of our age

by moving within the lives of those who believe.
> *Let even the rulers of the nations*
> *come under the pervasive influence*
> *of your peace and your love,*
> *that the senseless struggles of men*
> *may be brought to an end,*
> *and that the shadows*
> *that hang ominously over us*
> *may be dissolved.*

Look especially to those who need you greatly,
the helpless,
the bewildered,
those who suffer pain
and anguish of heart and soul,
those who languish in institutions.

> *Be with those of our number*
> *who are in far places,*
> *our service men and women,*
> *our college and university students,*
> *and all our young.*
> *Bless all lawful occupations,*
> *and cause us so to live*
> *that we will make clear our conviction*
> *that all belongs to you.*

These things we ask,
through your son and our savior, Jesus Christ,
who lives and rules with you and the Spirit,
one God forever. Amen.

II

Shorter Prayers of General Purpose

21

O God,
our refuge and our strength,
we praise you for life and all the substance of life,
for your love and grace
given to us without our deserving,
for the opportunities and challenges you set before us
that we may do your will.
> *Look in mercy upon all of our world,*
> *and according to our needs,*
> *visit and redeem us.*
> *Turn evil men from their wrong intentions,*
> *feed the hungry,*
> *comfort the diseased,*
> *send peace.*

Cause justice and virtue to prevail everywhere,
make our homes nurseries of your truth,
bless all lawful occupations.
Strengthen the church and give her the mind of Christ,
that men may see her Lord in her ministers and people.
> *So walk with us that our lives may reflect that Lord,*
> *Jesus Christ, your son and our savior,*
> *who lives and rules with you and the Spirit,*
> *one God forever. Amen.*

22

Almighty God, eternal Lord,
we praise you for your love
and ask for your continuing favor.
Look upon our human need,
and touch us with your healing hand.
Help us to live in peace
and prosper us in our honest pursuits.
Sustain any who suffer because of their faith,
and be the physician of the sick
and the mighty defense of the distraught.
> *Uphold your church in every place,*
> *and give us the will to give of ourselves*
> *for the building of your kingdom.*
> *Pour upon us a new measure of your Spirit,*
> *that we may rise above our apathy*
> *so as to assume greater measures of responsibility*
> *for the service of others.*

Give us,
O God,
comfort and consolation,
the zest of life and the courage of faith,
until that day when in mercy
you call us to be with you forever,
through Jesus Christ, your son, our Lord,
who lives and rules with you and the Spirit,
one God forever. Amen.

23

O eternal God,
our creator and our redeemer,
you have looked upon us in love,
and through the gift of your son Jesus Christ
you have become as one with us
that our lives may have new meaning.
For this we offer you our thanks,
and tell you of our hope that we may reflect your love for us
by our committed service to your people everywhere.

> *Look upon any who need you greatly.*
> *Give sustenance to the distressed and poverty-stricken.*
> *Uphold those who fight for truth.*
> *Shelter the weak and the sick,*
> *and give the sorrowing a new faith in the life eternal.*
> *Be the companion of those who travel,*
> *and those we love who are far distant from us.*
> *Help those who are perplexed*
> *to more clearly see your will.*

Let the leaders of the nations be people who desire peace.
Give new zeal to your church
that in all of her congregations and agencies
men may see the influence of Christ.
Fill us with a new awareness of his power for our lives,
that we may acknowledge him as our Lord,
who lives and rules with you and the Spirit,
one God forever. Amen.

24

Eternal God and Lord,
we praise you for your love,
for the promise of life and its purpose,
for your son, our savior, Jesus Christ.
> *Give us grace that we may live for him*
> *as we live for others,*
> *and hasten the coming of his kingdom*
> *of virtue and grace.*

Reach in mercy,
O God,
to places of desperation and hatred,
cruelty and violence.
Still the guns of war,
give sustenance to the poor,
guide those entrusted with grave responsibilities,
encourage the young,
comfort the sorrowing,
uphold the sick,
build your church.

> *Where walls of race or creed or nationality*
> *rise high between your people,*
> *break down those walls*
> *and unite all men as one.*
> *Bless the arts of men,*
> *and let freedom grow.*

Give us your joy,
even as you have given us the Lord of our lives,
Jesus Christ,
who lives and rules with you and the Spirit,
one God forever. Amen.

25

Eternal God,
the father of our Lord Jesus Christ,
we praise you for your love as revealed in Christ,
who loved us enough to suffer the humiliation of the cross.
We find meaning for our lives in his perfect life,
and we hold him as our master and Lord.

> *Work within us, we pray,*
> *so that we may be more like him.*
> *Help us to take upon ourselves*
> *the burdens of service for others, in his name.*
> *Help us to stand firm for truth*
> *despite the cost, in his name.*
> *Help us to live in love for all others*
> *even if they answer with hate, in his name.*

Gird the church with new zeal,
that men everywhere may hear the gospel,
that the lesson of the cross of Christ
may spread to every part of the world.
Cause peace among men and nations
to become a reality in this time,
and look upon all misfortune and need
with loving kindness and favor.

> *Grant that we may walk with Christ,*
> *that all of life might be lived in his presence,*
> *who lives and rules with you and the Spirit,*
> *one God forever. Amen.*

26

Lord God, our father,
you sent to our world the savior,
your son Jesus Christ.
He is our hope and our light,
the very prince of peace.
Cause us, by your Spirit,
to receive him anew in our lives.
By his love may we be led from despair to hope,
from emptiness to fulfillment,
from our bleak midwinters to new seasons of life and joy.
> *Receive,*
> *O God,*
> *the ancient cries of your people in every place.*
> *Reach to all our needs.*
> *Calm the tensions and correct the evils that lead to war.*
> *Make our church the very body of Christ,*
> *that our oneness may be evidence of our love*
> *and token of your Spirit's work among us.*

Praise be to you,
Lord God all-powerful,
through Jesus Christ, your son, our savior,
who lives and rules with you and the Spirit,
one God forever. Amen.

27

Eternal God, our father,
we praise you for your mercies new each day,
for your love in our creation and preservation,
for the gift of all gifts in your son,
our savior Jesus Christ.
> *Make us sensible of your benefits,*
> *O Lord,*
> *and cause your Spirit so to move within us*
> *that all we do may resound to your glory.*

Look upon human need,
dear father,
and give to such as are impoverished
the necessities of life,
while consoling those who are afflicted or downcast.
Prosper lawful occupations,
guide rulers in their work,
uphold your church and her pastors and people.

> *Strengthen us, we pray,*
> *that we will so give of ourselves to your kingdom*
> *that even the threats of this world shall not prevail.*
> *Thus may we hold faith*
> *with him who was a man for others,*
> *even Jesus Christ, your son, our savior,*
> *who lives and rules with you and the Spirit,*
> *one God forever. Amen.*

III

Prayers for the Church Year

28 ADVENT

Come, Lord Jesus. Come quickly.
Come to your people who suffer pain,
to the sick and the deformed,
to the persecuted and the beaten-down,
to the losers and the unlucky,
to the dull and the mistaken,
to the left-out and the forgotten,
to your people, Lord Jesus.
Come quickly.
> *Come to where men still fight battles,*
> *to where planes take off with their burdens of death,*
> *to soldiers tired and dirty and afraid,*
> *to lonely sentinels in unfriendly outposts;*
> *to sailors and marines and mechanics*
> *and riflemen and paratroopers and clerks,*
> *to the wounded and dying victims of our folly,*
> *to your people, Lord Jesus.*
> *Come quickly.*

Come to the old and the feeble,
to the poor and the exploited,
to those imprisoned because of political crimes,
to those imprisoned because they have stolen or murdered,
to those imprisoned without cause,
to lost children and abandoned infants,
to any anywhere who cannot laugh,
to your people, Lord Jesus.
Come quickly.

Come to your church, to your body on earth,
to the officials and the leaders,
to the boards and agencies,
to the institutions of education and service,
to the congregations large and small,
to the people, some faithful and some indifferent,
to the people, some virtuous and some evil,
to the people, some humble and some proud,
to your people in your church, Lord Jesus.
Come quickly.
You are light in the darkness of our world.
You bring peace, and joy, and love.
You are hope, and promise, and future.
Come to your people, Lord Jesus.
Come quickly. Amen.

29   CHRISTMAS

Eternal Lord and father,
you are more powerful than we can describe,
and it is right that we give all honor and glory to you.
It is even presumptuous of us
to dare to address our prayers to you,
so great is the difference between us,
and yet you have given us the assurance of your presence
as well as instruction to turn to you
in prayer and supplication.
For this willingness to hear us, O God,
which we can scarcely understand,
we are grateful.

> *We thank you especially for your power,*
> *infinite and beyond all our definition,*
> *yet compressed into human flesh for our good.*
> *For this incredible concern*
> *made evident in Jesus Christ*
> *we give you the worship of our hearts*
> *and the service of our lives.*

Men called your son the prince of peace,
and so he is.
Grant, dear Lord,
that his peace may surround all of this holy season.
Cause human greed and selfishness to be stopped,
at least for these few days.
Touch with your pity every tragic condition in our world,
and ease sorrow and bitterness and tension.

*Give children everywhere a cause for joy,
and ease the unhappy results of poverty and ignorance
by advancing the cause of understanding,
charity, and good will.
Move the nations and their leaders
away from the desperate old paths
that have so often ended in bloody ways,
and teach us all those new and higher roads
that surely can represent our future.*
Turn your church away from whatever may prevent her
from proclaiming the good news of Christ.
Raise up within her scores of dedicated people
who will run from Bethlehem's stable
to tell others that the Lord is at hand.
Give us the grace,
O God,
to live our days in that same light,
through your son Jesus Christ,
who is our chief joy and our only Lord,
with you and the Spirit,
one God forever. Amen.

30   CHRISTMAS

O God, our father,
we are your children,
fashioned because of your love for us,
born to life in this good world
and called to serve you by serving one another.
For our very life,
> *we give you our thanks.*

We believe,
father,
that you gave us your son,
Jesus Christ.
We believe he became like us,
of human flesh and blood,
a child in the arms of his mother.
We believe he is the prince of peace,
and for his coming,
> *we give you our thanks.*

Let his peace come alive
in all the troubled parts of our world.
Quiet the selfish cries of selfish men
who would have us hate our brothers.
Bring us to trust in him and in one another
so that we will beat our swords into plowshares,
disarming our warheads,
mustering out our armies,
and redirecting our economy to the things of peace.
> *We ask you to help us, good Lord.*

Look in pity upon any of your children in their need,
those who wander without homes or shelter,
those who fear the cold and damp,
those who are hungry and sick and unhappy.
> *We ask you to help them, good Lord.*

Give new evidence of your love
to those who feel abandoned and alone.
Consider the plight of the refugees,
the unemployed,
the imprisoned,
the persecuted,
the outcast,
the disenfranchised.
Reach in pity to any who search for meaning
and fail to find it.
> *We ask you to help them, good Lord.*

Be the God of all our human ways
and where they are ways of justice,
preserve them.
Where they are ways of inequity,
destroy them.
Move in and through our institutions,
our churches and schools,
our commerce and industry,
our governments and our structures,
and bend them to your will.
Overcome our inertia and our apathy
and propel us into new avenues
of responsible participation within society.
> *We ask you to help us, good Lord.*

Give us joy,
O father,
greater than the fleeting joys of this present world,
the joy of those who have seen light in great darkness.
With men of old
may we come and adore the newborn king,
even Jesus Christ, your son, our savior,
who lives and rules with you and the Spirit,
one God forever. Amen.

31   LENT

O Lord Jesus Christ,
you set your face to Jerusalem, long ago,
determined to walk the road to that city
even though its end would be the cross.
We thank you for your concern reaching even to death.
Walk with us, we pray,
as we try to follow paths of service and sacrifice.
Restrain us should we seek to parade our piety,
and direct us into avenues of devotion
which reflect your love.
Strengthen us to live for others.

> *Look upon all human need,*
> *and give to your people, the church,*
> *the vigor needed for the tasks at hand.*
> *Be a continuing presence to your people*
> *who are in special need,*
> *the sick, the anxious, the sorrowing.*

> *Grant peace to our world,*
> *and encourage those who seek a more humane society.*

And give us,
O Christ,
faith in you and in your purposes for us.
Make us bold to speak your truth
when others elect the safety of silence.
Make us foolish enough to live

for the least of your brothers
when others are living for themselves.
Make us forget ourselves by remembering
your life and death and resurrection.
You live and rule with the father and the Spirit,
one God forever. Amen.

32   LENT

Here we are again,
O God,
daring to pray to you
even though we often continue to wonder
if you really exist;
presuming to beg your guidance for our lives
even though we have little intention
of changing what we do;
piously calling your attention
to the needy of our world
while adding to our own
overfed, overclothed overabundance.
The wonder is that you do not lose patience with us.
You continue to love us,
and the cross of your son continues to speak
to our insipid and arrogant sin,
and for this we are grateful.
Help us,
Lord God,
to increasingly demonstrate
the fruits of thankfulness,
that our treasure and talent and time
may be consecrated to your will and your people.
> *Our world still hovers*
> *on the brink of destruction,*
> *father.*
> *The swift and terrible tragedies*

that strike at us but underscore our need for you.
Look upon those in despair and sorrow,
and give them your grace.
Heal, by your mercy and will, the sick.
Give strength to all who suffer for your truth.

Keep the bitter memory of conflict and war so fresh in our minds
that even as we think of those who serve
in the armed forces of our country
we may also be determined to create
a society without guns and soldiers.
Guide rulers everywhere,
that they may seek peace and pursue it.
Be our peace here as a people,
and our hope,
and our Lord.
> *Give us, now, the heart to go from here in love,*
> *to walk among men in our world*
> *in the image of your son,*
> *even Jesus Christ, our savior,*
> *who lives and rules with you and the Spirit,*
> *one God forever. Amen.*

33 PALM SUNDAY

Lord God eternal,
we are far removed from the day
when people loudly welcomed Jesus into Jerusalem.
Even when we are gathered in your name
we give you but a portion of our lives.
Yet you have loved us
beyond our deserving.
In Christ you have given us a savior
instead of the judge we have earned.
> *We are grateful for your love.*
> *Work within us that some of the cynical wisdom*
> *of our generation may be replaced with simple trust.*
> *Help us to love you,*
> *and to find expression of that love*
> *in our concern for your people.*

Be with all sorts and conditions of men.
Look to the needy of our world,
those held down by poverty and deprivation,
weakened by inadequate food or shelter,
crushed in spirit by inequities and denials of freedom.
> *As Christ came to the city of Jerusalem,*
> *let him enter upon our cities.*
> *Give his people courage*
> *to speak for those who are oppressed,*
> *impatience with dishonesty*
> *and corruption in high places,*
> *zeal to take up whips*

and drive out those
    who live only for their own advantage.
Continue to be the Lord of your church.
Awaken in us a sense of obligation
toward those who are not within the body of Christ.
Guide us to whatever new means may be needed
to tell of his love with understanding,
and make us willing to relinquish
what we cherish most in our heritage
if it causes any to refuse the gospel.
   Whatever else you see that we need,
   father,
   grant to us.
   Give peace between nations and between neighbors.
   Uphold those who suffer sickness and adversity,
   and comfort those who sorrow.

Be the companion of those we love who are far from us.
Grant that we may know the peace which the world cannot give,
through our faith in the prince of peace,
your son, Jesus Christ, our Lord,
who lives and rules with you and the Spirit,
one God forever. Amen.

34 HOLY WEEK

Dear Lord,
we are forever trying to understand,
forever searching for lost treasure,
forever contending with our lives and our times.
See us even now
as we wonder what we are
and what we are about.
Come and help us with your truth
and build us up by your love.
> *Caring about ourselves,*
> *we do not care very much for others.*
> *We turn our backs upon the poor.*
> *We laugh at the awkward, the confused, the weak.*
> *We do not listen to the outraged cries*
> *of those who contend for peace and justice.*
> *See us in our indifference and pride,*
> *and give us a new determination*
> *to live for Christ*
> *by living for others.*

Rule in your world,
O God.
Set straight those who control the lives of others,
officials and employers
and authorities and professionals,
and give us all a sense of our responsibility
to one another.
Hold before us the example of Christ,

that as he determined to do what must be done,
we may live with such resolve,
in his name,
who lives and rules with you and the Spirit,
one God forever. Amen.

35   HOLY WEEK

O Lord,
we remember you,
and the last week of your life on earth.
You were taken by evil men,
scorned and tortured,
unjustly condemned,
and put to death.
> *Sometimes we are badly used too,*
> *and wrongs done to us*
> *are never righted.*
>> *Sometimes*
>> *we are the killers of men's dreams,*
>> *Herods playing cynical games,*
>> *high priests manipulating other's lives,*
>> *Judases buying blood.*

Forgive us for our times of treachery,
deceit and intolerance.
Give us the strength to endure
when crosses loom large in our lives.
> *See your world and your people,*
> *still given to violent answers,*
> *still destroying the good*
> *in the name of expediency,*
> *still afraid of truth.*
>> *Come to our world.*
>> *Come to your people.*
>> *Turn men and nations away*

from their reliance upon weapons and war.
Quiet the preachers of bigotry and hatred.
Uphold the guardians of virtue and justice.
Reach in love to the unloved and the loveless,
and as there are those we hold dear who need you,
come with your peace to them.

Work through us as a community of your people,
that we may find ways of bringing truth
to our society,
healing to broken lives,
and help to human need.
Deepen the kinship we share
because of our faith in you,
that believing you died for us,
we may live for one another
with greater commitment and trust.
We pray,
dear Jesus,
in your name and as your people.   Amen.

36 EASTER

Eternal God and Lord,
by your power even death has died,
and we rejoice in the new life won by Jesus Christ.
The arrogance of cruel men,
the timidity of frightened disciples,
the injustice of mindless crowds,
all are now overcome
and wrongs are righted,
and we can believe in the future.
For this we praise you,
and pledge you our very lives.
> *See where death continues to hold dominion,*
> *father,*
> *and work new resurrections,*
> *using us as instruments of your power.*
> *Renew our confidence in your coming kingdom.*
> *Where we falter with discouragement enlarge our faith.*
> *Where our vision is small, show us your will.*

And so may it be that the new life of Christ
is the life of our world,
for the age of peace and brotherhood and love.
So may it be. Amen.

EASTER

O Lord,
dare we believe what we are told about you?
> *Are you alive,*
> *or is this story only the invention*
> *of imaginative men?*

Have you won your battle
against hatred and selfishness and death,
or are they still our enemies and our fate?
> *Do we live, now,*
> *as citizens of your kingdom,*
> *gathered as your people,*
> *or are we here by mistake,*
> *praying to a fraud?*

Dare we believe what we are told about you,
Lord?
We dare to believe.
Help us when we do not believe.
> *And help us live as we believe.*
> *Because you are alive and set loose in our world,*
> *make us alive and reckless of ourselves*
> *for the sake of your truth*
> *and for the love of your people.*

Go with us into the places of death
that we might bring resurrection.
Transform all of your people by your power
that injustice and cruelty,
poverty and despair,

arrogance and war,
and all the terrible forces of death
may be overcome,
destroyed,
forever set aside.
> *We believe in you,*
> *O risen Lord.*
> *Help us when we do not believe. Amen.*

38 PENTECOST

O Spirit of God,
you are a fire cleansing and consuming,
> *you are a dove coming from on high,*

you are a still small voice,
> *you are everywhere,*

you are in us and about us,
> *you have prompted our faith,*

you have suggested our good works,
> *you have formed us into your people,*

you have built the church on earth,
> *you are a fire,*

you are a dove,
> *you are a still small voice,*

and we listen for you and we follow you,
lest we turn aside into the ways of darkness.
> *Move in and through your church.*
> *Set it to the preaching of the gospel*
> *and the doing of your will.*
> *Where it is narrow, enlarge its vision.*
> *Where it is weary, restore its strength.*
> *Where it is wrong, give it sense.*

Surge within the lives of your people in every place.
Spur them to visit the sick and the imprisoned,
to care for the needy and the underprivileged,
to right the wrongs done by the accidents of life,
to encourage each other in the doing of love.

Even when men refuse to believe,
work within them to the good of others.
Be the power behind all thrones
and offices and headquarters.
Be the thrust of society,
  a force for the virtues of our race.
And set us,
God,
to reaching for high goals,
to noble and helpful purposes,
to the improvement of our world
and the improvement of our lives.
Prevent us from being discouraged,
and let us see visions of the world as it could be,
in peace and prosperity
by commitment to Jesus Christ,
who lives and rules with you and the father,
one God forever. Amen.

39 THANKSGIVING

O father,
we are far removed from those
who first determined to set aside
a time of giving thanks.
We have so much, and they had so little.
Our tastes are jaded, our stomachs full,
our lives a silly race for getting more and more.
> *Have you been too good to us,*
> *father?*
> *Though we own the bounty of this earth*
> *in measure beyond the counting,*
> *still we complain a lot,*
> *hoard our treasures,*
> *and persist in believing that everything*
> *that really matters*
> *is related to getting*
> *and keeping*
> *and saving*
> *and spending.*

It is such a dreary routine.
Surely, long ago, when they set aside this time
for giving thanks
it did not seem so hollow.
> *Restore us,*
> *O God.*
> *Remind us, as we give our thanks*
> *for turkey and stuffing and potatoes and pie,*

that millions are grateful for crusts.
Even today, when our grain elevators,
our supermarkets, our freezers,
our ovens, and our plates are full,
millions are grateful for crusts.
Good God!
How can we give our thanks in the midst of too much?
Wake us up, and soften us up,
and make us decent again.
We are fat and flabby
and obscene with plenty.
Make us human with concern.
Spread your blessings among all the people.
Even up the have's and the have-not's of your world.
Bring the rich and the mighty down
and bring up the beggars at their gates
that they may share equally in the good of life.
And let it be,
father,
that we give our thanks for important things,
for life,
for one another,
for smiles, and hope, and love,
and for Jesus Christ.
He is our joy, and our hope, and our love,
and we pray in his name. Amen.

40 Last Sunday After PENTECOST

Our father God,
in this world all things change and pass away,
but you are forever.
Our seasons seem only moments,
but you are beyond our time.
See us as we are.
See our weakness, our confusion, our wandering,
and come to us with your love.

> *Come to us in Christ.*
> *Challenge us by the example of his life*
> *given for all the world.*
> *Show us where he lives today*
> *waiting to be served by us,*
> *and show us how he can come alive*
> *as we come alive with his love.*
> *Quiet the restless striving of our world.*
> *Redirect those who worship profit,*
> *awaken those who live for their senses,*
> *encourage those who live in fear for the future.*

See our people in their need for you.
See our friends, our families, our neighbors.
By your will give health to the sick and infirm,
peace and understanding to the sorrowing,
assurance to the nervous and distracted.

> *See all the people of our world,*
> *father.*

See the poor, the rich, the wise, the foolish.
See the directors of industry,
the rulers of governments and the leaders of armies,
see the bishops and priests and pastors,
see the enslaved and embittered and deluded,
see all the people of our world
and come to them with your love.
Mend our divisions.
Help us to forget the wrongs
that have been done to us.
Point out to us the folly of our hatreds,
and remind us of the brevity of life
that we may add to its beauty
and share in its light.

For all who have lived,
we give our thanks.
For our ancestors and our associates
and our special loves
who have lived and died,
we give our thanks.
And for Jesus Christ,
who is our life and our hope,
we give our thanks.

Direct us, in these last days,
that we may live as he lived,
by giving ourselves to others.
Uphold us, in these last days,
by our faith in him,
who lives and rules with you and the Spirit,
one God forever. Amen.

IV

Prayers for the Secular Seasons

41 New Year

O eternal God,
a year is done, and another begins.
We remember what has been.
We wonder about what will be.
Will we succeed or fail?
Will we be happy or sad?
Will we live or die?
Our times are in your hands,
as all of our past has been in your company,
and though we look to the future with fear
and are reluctant to walk the unknown path,
yet we are sure of you.
We believe that in your care all will be well.

> *So many of your people stand in need,*
> *dear Lord.*
> *See them where they suffer for the lack of food,*
> *see them struggling for life in bad housing,*
> *see them wrapping rags around their bodies for warmth,*
> *and help us to see them too,*
> *that we may be your arms of love*
> *reaching to their needs.*
> *See your people where they are handicapped*
> *in body and mind,*
> *see them where they are deprived of their rights,*
> *see them where they are captives of superstition,*
> *ignorance, and prejudice.*
> *Help us to see them too,*

*that we may be your arms of love
reaching to their needs.
See your people where they do not know of Christ,
see them where they know him but do not follow him,
see them where they worship gods of power
and comfort and prestige and propriety.
Help us to see them too,
that we may be your arms of love
reaching to their needs.*
Look especially, we pray,
upon those of our number for whom we care greatly,
the disillusioned, the despondent,
the confined, the saddened, the ill,
and grant them peace.

*Be the God of our institutions and associations,
and of our relationships with each other.
Work in your church
to the coming of your kingdom.
Bless our homes with your presence,
give our schools new relevence for these times,
keep our corporations and unions and cooperatives
mindful of the needs of all people,
honest and efficient.*
Be the ruler of all rulers everywhere,
and counsel those set over us,
the leaders of this city,
the governor of this state,
the president of this nation.

Cause this to be the year,
O God,
when peace comes forever to our earth,
when soldiers of every nation return to their homes,
when guns begin to rust,
when warheads are dismantled,
when industry is geared to life.
Let peace come this year,
O God.
Let peace come this year.
Father, hear us.
Bring a new beginning to our old commitments.
Awaken us to the work you have for us in this year,
and help us to live for one another,
as Jesus Christ lived for us,
who lives and rules with you and the Spirit,
one God forever. Amen.

42 Winter

Father,
this morning's weather is so bad
most of your people never left their homes,
and the few of us who did come
are in danger of thinking too highly of ourselves,
as if we could define our Christianity
by our willingness to drive to church
on a slippery street.
> *Forgive us if we've had this notion.*
> *Help us to be more charitable with the absent.*
> *Remind us of what real sacrifice is all about,*
> *and when our chances come to be brave*
> *keep us faithful.*

Look today upon any who are being hurt
by storms and cold and floods and natural disasters.
Work through your people in every place,
that they may in your name mercifully reach to the distressed
with food and medicine and clothing and shelter.
> *We are concerned especially about those we know,*
> *our friends and our families and our neighbors,*
> *those who share with us in this fellowship of faith.*
> *Some are not well,*
> *and some are discouraged and confused,*
> *and some are desperate because of misfortune.*
> *Be what is needed, dear Lord,*
> *physician, teacher, counselor, friend,*
> *and show us how we can take these parts ourselves.*

Be the companion of those who must work in this season,
bus drivers, pilots, engineers, truck drivers,
mailmen, delivery people, linemen, refuse collectors,
policemen and firemen,
and prosper by your grace all our vocations.
Remember our young people,
and give them hope for a better world
while preparing them for life as it really is today.
Protect our service men and women,
especially those who face danger and death,
and speed the day when men no longer go to war.
> *O Lord,*
> *we know that the quality of our leadership*
> *is directly related to the degree of our involvement,*
> *in our schools and churches,*
> *in our neighborhoods and our communities,*
> *in our corporations and labor unions.*
> *Rouse us from our comfort and our warmth.*
> *Cure us of our apathy.*
> *Open our eyes to the ways we can become committed,*
> *and so through us create pieces of your kingdom*
> *in our earthly institutions.*

Be with us as a people called together in your service.
Give us a new sense of our unity,
even when it is far from visible,
and a new determination to love one another,
even as we have been loved by Jesus Christ. Amen.

43   Spring

We are in the season when life returns,
father.
> *The grass is greening under our feet.*
> *Flowers are spreading their pleasant colors.*
> *Even the pace of things has changed,*
> *and we pause, now and again,*
> *and let our business wait for the sake of*
> *the sights and the sounds and the smells.*

It is the spring of the year,
and we are grateful for its joy and its promise.
> *Some places will not know a spring this year,*
> *Lord.*
> *Wars scorch your green earth,*
> *and the tears of those who survive*
> *are too bitter for the soil.*
> *Refugees swell highways*
> *and swarm over vacant fields*
> *longing for their homes,*
> *but knowing only squallor and disease and despair.*
> *Through all our world*
> *a few have much*
> *and many have nothing*
> *and the gulf widens.*
> *What can your people do about*
> *these monstrous wrongs, O Lord?*
> *Give us your word for these times.*

Some cannot see the loveliness of this season, father.

They are ill or infirm,
or they are distracted by the hurt of a recent sorrow,
or they are confused by the madness of our society.
Look to their needs.
Reach to them with your love.
Give them hope.

> *Work your newness through all of our lives,*
> *into our institutions and our professions,*
> *into our commerce and our industry,*
> *into our homes and our schools,*
> *into our governments and our churches.*
> *Where people are enslaved*
> *because of tradition or prejudice or sin,*
> *be their power,*
> *and to that end use us.*
> *Be the power within us,*
> *for the freedom of all your people.*

For we believe,
father,
that you intend us to be free,
even as you sent your son,
Jesus Christ,
to gain our freedom.
He lives and rules
with you and the Spirit,
one God forever. Amen.

44 Summer

Forgive us,
Lord,
for the restlessness and the wandering minds
that mark our worship of you in this season.
Maybe we are oppressed by the heat,
wearied by the humidity,
or lacking in enthusiasm
because so many people are away
and there are dozens of empty spaces.
> *We know that we should praise you*
> *as if this were Easter Sunday*
> *or Christmas Eve.*
> *Instead it's only the same old thing.*
> *Help us now,*
> *O God,*
> *to joy in your presence and your love,*
> *as well as when we are many*
> *and the day is very special.*

Reach to our needs,
dear father.
Remember those for whom discomfort is a particular burden
because of the weather,
the sick, the weak,
the pressured and the confused.
See the sorrow in the hearts of many,
and give them peace.
Uphold those who are brave enough

to live out their faith in you,
and frustrate the designs of evil men.

> *Where there is war in our world,*
> *bring sense and reconciliation.*
> *Where there is injustice and oppression,*
> *bigotry and selfishness,*
> *bring the victory of truth and virtue.*
> *Where men no longer care for themselves*
> *or for others,*
> *rescue them from their apathy*
> *and encourage them to new measures of devotion.*

Look to those who in this season
have special reason to be concerned about their welfare.
Give sun and rain to the farmer,
warmth and light to the vacationer,
recreation to those worn by the cares of life,
patience to those stalled in traffic,
the memory of your love to those who would forget you,
and to us all a new understanding of your son
and his gift to us, even life itself,
through the same Jesus Christ, our Lord,
who lives and rules with you and the Spirit,
one God forever. Amen.

45 Fall

Our God and father,
all around we see signs of the dying of the year.
Farmers are gathering their harvests,
leaves are turning and falling,
we are much concerned with storm windows
and snow tires and warmer clothing.
> *Yet there is beauty in this time,*
> *as in all of your times.*
> *The colors of this season,*
> *the crisp refreshment of the air,*
> *the taste of apples red from your sun,*
> *all remind us of your love.*
> *We know ourselves to be your own.*
> *We know we need not fear*
> *the coming of the winter.*

Look to your children who have particular concerns at this time:
students struggling with difficult assignments,
homeless men feeling the chill in the air
and wondering about shelter in the months ahead,
weak and infirm folk
who have relished the warmth of the summer,
workers employed only for the season past
who now search for jobs.
> *Reach to all of our needs by your love.*
> *Where we are cast down by worry*
> *restore us to a new hope,*
> *where we are in pain or affliction*

give us strength and patience,
where we are lost
help us to be found.

Come with your love to all the associations of men,
to our cities and towns,
our states and our nation.
Cause those who hold authority over us to be honest and wise,
and give them a mind to value peace above all else.
Enter into our homes,
fortify our families,
reform and restore our churches,
redirect our schools,
that in all the institutions of life
we may be informed by your Spirit
and determined to do your will.
Keep us close to you and to your truth,
committed to living in love with one another
in imitation of your son, our savior, Jesus Christ,
who lives and rules with you and the Spirit,
one God forever. Amen.

46 College Education

O Lord, our God and father,
you have made us and all that exists,
you care for us and all of your children,
you reach to us in our need
with the power of your love,
and for what we are and have,
because of your goodness,
we give you our thanks.
> *We are especially concerned,*
> *O father,*
> *about our young people*
> *as they begin another year of study.*
> *We love them,*
> *and desire that their lives*
> *be rich with useful service to our world*
> *and faithful devotion to you.*

Be with them as they go to their schools.
Guard their travel.
Encourage them to serious purposes
and open their minds
to new ideas and greater understanding.
Grant counselors and teachers and administrators
an increased sense of their responsibility
as molders of opinion and conviction.
> *See us as a people,*
> *dear God,*
> *and come to us in our need.*

Where we are narrow and intolerant,
where we are provincial and suspicious,
where we are fearful and embittered,
bring us to faith and love.
As any among us are in particular need
because of the infirmities of life,
reach with healing and help.

You are the Lord of the nations,
and all people everywhere should know you
as their God and father.
Cause the truth of your gospel
to come to those places that do not know your love.
Speak to those who hold in their hands
the destinies of others,
leaders of government and industry
and the social order.
Give them a desire to serve justly
and in freedom.
> *Bring peace to our world,*
> *O father.*
> *Bring peace.*

Go with us now into our different lives and vocations,
keeping us sensible of our unity in your love,
and grateful for your gift in Christ,
through whom we pray. Amen.

47 National Elections

O Lord, our God,
we have been much involved as a nation
with an examination of our times and our affairs.
We have been considering the events of the recent past
and our options for the immediate future.
In this process we have heard many promises
as well as many opinions,
and some exaggerations
and some untruths.
We are now almost to the time of decision,
and we need your help.
> *How else can we perceive fact from fancy?*
> *How else can we determine competence and sincerity?*
> *How else can we identify the issues*
> *now masked by advertising*
> *and slogans and personalities?*

Guide us as we cast our ballots.
Direct us,
that our votes may count for peace,
for justice,
for the relief of poverty,
for the rights of all your people in every place.
> *Nor let us believe,*
> *dear God,*
> *that we are fulfilling our responsibilities*
> *simply by participating in an election.*
> *If we are not now involved*

*in some work for the community,
show us what we can do.
Prompt us,
if we have the talent,
to political activity.
Open the doors to our greater service
in the process of government
and in other areas of society's life.
Bring your kingdom into our world,
and use us to that effect.*
O God,
as our leaders are determined
and courses of action are selected,
continue to be with us.
Uphold us when those leaders are in error
and those actions are harmful,
that we may have the wisdom to understand
and the courage to act.
If we are weak or fearful,
raise up prophets to correct us.
Sustain and encourage us when we are well governed
and our policies benefit the whole of our human family.
*So may it be that our nation is preserved,
not for our good above all others,
but as a good for all others.
We are, as your people, called to live
beyond ourselves.
Help us in that resolve
even as a nation.*
For we know ourselves,

by your love,
to have a kinship with your people
that goes beyond the claims of race and creed and nation.
Christ, our savior,
came for all of your people everywhere.
Hear this, our prayer, in his name. Amen.

48 Christmas Preparation

Eternal Lord and father,
the frenzy of the season surrounds us,
and our schedules are so full
we know we'll never get everything done.
We come to you in haste, distracted and tired.
Forgive us for what we have done to this time in the year.
Help us to remake our time,
that even if we never wrap the gifts,
or bake the cookies,
or send the cards,
we still may be ready for your son.

> *We know that he came to live for us,*
> *to show us how to live for others.*
> *Help us to learn his lessons well.*
> *Help us to be ministers of his truth and mercy.*
> *As we might have the opportunity,*
> *use us to heal the divisions between men,*
> *to stand for justice where the weak are threatened,*
> *to act with food and clothing and shelter*
> *where your children are poor.*

See us where we have gathered ourselves into families,
O God,
and as you looked in love upon Joseph and Mary,
look in love upon us.
Be with those we care for greatly who must travel soon,
and encourage such caution and watchfulness
that journies may be safe

and reunions happy.
Keep us from shortness of temper,
overindulgence in food and drink,
and lives so full with celebrating
we have no room for Christ.
> *Do not let us forget the lonely.*
> *In our concern to remember those*
> *who have remembered us,*
> *help us to think of those no one misses,*
> *and help us to find a way to let them know we care.*

Be with all of your people through all of your world.
Where your church is under oppression,
give her courage and help her to endure.
Where your church is soft with comfort,
awaken her to the demands of your gospel.
> *Be the companion of all manner of men,*
> *presidents and governors and mayors,*
> *teachers and students,*
> *farmers and laborers and craftsmen,*
> *housewives and secretaries,*
> *all in any place who need your help.*
> *Give to all people everywhere*
> *the knowledge of your love and truth.*

Come with your kingdom upon our earth.
Rule in our hearts, and in the hearts of all your people.
Establish peace, and be our peace,
through Jesus Christ, your son, our Lord. Amen.

V

Prayers Especially for Use when Communion is Offered

Most of the prayers in this book could appropriately be used when the sacrament is given, but those contained in this section include specific reference to the Lord's Supper.

49 COMMUNION

O father,
we are the lost found by your grace,
we are the torn asunder made whole by your hand.
For all you have done and given and been,
we thank you and praise you.
> *Undergird us in our resolves,*
> *that in our devotion to you*
> *we may see the prices waiting to be paid,*
> *and losing our fears,*
> *proceed to pay them.*
> *So may it be that the hungry are fed,*
> *the naked clothed,*
> *the homeless housed.*
> *So may it be that injustice is corrected,*
> *bigotry overcome,*
> *hypocrisy exposed.*
> *So may it be that our government*
> *is the servant of the people,*
> *peace a lasting reality,*
> *and the society of the future*
> *rich with human values.*
> *So may it be,*
> *Lord,*
> *by your love active in us.*

Where the needs of our world
are beyond our ministry,
work through men everywhere

to the accomplishment of your good will.
Be the companion of the lonely
and the strength of the oppressed.
Give your church a new dimension of life,
and cause useful arts and occupations
to flourish among us.
> *Live in us,*
> *to the redemption of your world.*
> *Live in us,*
> *that our lives may be the life of Jesus Christ,*
> *given for others,*
> *who lives and rules with you and the Spirit,*
> *one God forever. Amen.*

COMMUNION

Dear Lord,
as you have given us instruction,
we come to you,
confident of your love for us,
trusting in you,
knowing that you have promised to be with us always,
even to the end of this world.
> *So often we do not remember that you are with us.*
> *Intent upon our own designs,*
> *we get caught up by the rush of things,*
> *made nervous and tense by pressures,*
> *confused by all that competes for our attention.*

How grateful we are to be able to come together in communion
with each other and with you.
Restore us,
O Jesus,
and give us your strength.
> *Look upon those who need you greatly.*
> *And, as it is your will, reach to their needs.*

> *Move in and through our society*
> *with your freedom and your truth.*
> *Where violence and war prevail,*
> *cause men of goodwill to exert their efforts*
> *for the building of peace.*

Remind us that we are your people.

When we are tempted to go our separate ways,
draw us close, one to another.
> *Save us from becoming an island*
> *set apart from the world.*
> *Bring us together*
> *that we may be more determined*
> *to go forth and serve.*
So may it be that we are your love for the world
because we give ourselves to the world,
as you gave yourself for us. Amen.

51 COMMUNION

O Lord,
how good it is to be here.
We know we are as one because of your love,
and we find new strength in one another.
We uphold each other, in adversity, in pain,
in discouragement and defeat,
and you give us this wonderful ability
to be your ministers in the world
and in your church.
> *Don't let us grow indifferent to our power,*
> *father.*
> *Don't let us take one another for granted.*
> *Don't let us make a mockery of your love*
> *by being selfish or cruel.*

Instead work through us to an even greater extent
so that your people may be served.
Especially, we pray, give us compassion and insight
for the sake of the sick, the lost, the alone, the sad.

> *Make your world what it ought to be,*
> *and use us as instruments of your peace.*
> *Make your people what they ought to be,*
> *starting with us,*
> *and use us as instruments of your peace.*

And make your church what it ought to be,
your people gathered

to hear your word and share your love,
and equip us for the doing of your will
in all the world,
through Jesus Christ, your son, our Lord,
who lives and rules with you and the Spirit,
one God forever. Amen.

52 COMMUNION

Gracious God,
we know you care about us,
and that you have called us together
much as a father calls to himself his family.
We are your own,
and we follow your son, Jesus.
> *Be with us now,*
> *and at all the times of life,*
> *that how we live and what we say*
> *may reflect what we believe about you.*

Many need you greatly because of the special situations
of their lives,
sickness, pain, discouragement, sorrow.
Look upon them in their need,
reach to them with your love,
and uphold them by your grace.

> *We thank you for those who lead*
> *and guide us in this life,*
> *for magistrates and rulers,*
> *for teachers and counselors.*
> *Lead and guide them, we pray,*
> *and let peace come to our earth and her people.*

See your children in all their places and conditions,
O Lord,
and prosper them in their lawful occupations

and encourage them when they seek to serve you.
Bless your church,
and strengthen the young
and give us a sense of meaning for our lives,
in that we know ourselves to be your servants.
> *These things we pray in the name of Jesus Christ,*
> *your son, our Lord,*
> *who lives and rules with you and the Spirit,*
> *one God forever. Amen.*

53 COMMUNION

Eternal God, our father,
we are called to live as did Jesus,
becoming like him through the places and times of life,
constructing what we can of his kingdom.
As you support us with strength equal to our task,
as you preserve us from ourselves,
we give you our thanks and praise.
Continue your love,
O God,
by saving us from our selfish ways,
that in losing ourselves we may be found.

> *Surround with your care the ill and the lonely,*
> *those who are in the depths of sorrow,*
> *those who have lost their way.*
> *Frustrate evil men who would profit*
> *by the misfortunes of others.*
> *Guide your people in all the walks of life,*
> *that in commerce and industry,*
> *in the professions and in the trades,*
> *in the workings of government*
> *and in the avenues of social service,*
> *there may be honesty and devotion*
> *above the cause of personal gain.*

Give direction to those who are set over us,
the mayor of this city,
the governor of this state,
the president of this nation.

Bless our countrymen who may be engaged in battle,
and bless our enemies,
and bring all wars to an end,
that we may live in peace and justice.
> *Make us more anxious to serve*
> *than to be served,*
> *more ready to give of ourselves*
> *and less intent upon receiving,*
> *as was him who gave his body and blood*
> *that we may be strengthened and preserved*
> *unto eternal life,*
> *Jesus Christ, your son, our Lord,*
> *who lives and rules with you and the Spirit,*
> *one God forever. Amen.*

54 COMMUNION

Eternal father,
we are come together as your family,
sharing your love
and our kinship, one to another,
as your children.
> *We know your will, that we be one,*
> *and we know that our oneness is not complete.*
> *Others of your children in other places*
> *are aliens and strangers to us.*
> *Sickness, adversity, and distance*
> *have separated us from some*
> *in this family of faith.*
> *And some are not reconciled,*
> *one to another.*

Take our differences,
Lord,
our separations and self-interests,
our variety and distinction and disagreement,
and make us one by the receiving of your love.
Take our lives, and make them your life
alive in our world.
So may it be that the divisions among men
dissolve by the power of your presence,
through Jesus Christ, your son, our Lord,
who lives and rules with you and the Spirit,
one God forever. Amen.

VI

Prayers for Other Purposes

55 Family

O gracious God,
by your mercy we take our every breath.
> *We are made in your image.*
> *You set the solitary in families*
> *and set free those who are bound with chains.*

We praise you with all we are,
and pray for your continuing help,
so that what we are
may more fully reflect your love for us.
> *Cause us,*
> *O God,*
> *to have a concern for others,*
> *as did Jesus Christ.*
> *We see the needs of others in our world*
> *and insist that they are greater than we can meet.*
> *Show us what we can do.*

Work in us so that through us
there may come relief from the despair of poverty,
learning for those now held under by ignorance,
release for those who are unjustly imprisoned,
and liberty for those living in oppression.
> *Nor let us believe,*
> *father,*
> *that human need exists only on other shores.*
> *Help us to see the ways*
> *we can help our neighbors,*
> *and the members of our families.*

Build our homes into strongholds of faith,
and your church into your kingdom here on earth.
Grant that both home and church
may be adequate to the pressures of our age.
Cause all useful occupations to flourish,
and guide our leaders into the ways of peace.
And make us,
O God,
more like Christ:
Give us a new measure of sincerity
in our dealings with others,
a new measure of insight
upon the things that matter most,
a new measure of willingness
to rejoice in the day
and fear not for the future.
And more than all else,
let the love of Christ
be the power that moves within us,
to his glory and to the good of your people,
through the same Jesus Christ, your son, our savior,
who lives and rules with you and the Spirit,
one God forever. Amen.

56   A Time of Tragedy and Shock

Our God and father,
we are in despair and sorrow.
Because we trust in you, and know you care,
we turn to you now and share with you our trouble.

> *Reach to us in our need, father.*
> *Come with fresh assurance of your love.*
> *Touch us with healing and hope.*

See your people in any place who need you.
Feed the hungry and clothe the naked.
Shelter the homeless and comfort the anguished.
Turn aside the evil of cruel men,
and frustrate those who would take advantage of the weak.

> *Give your church the insight and strength*
> *to go to your people with love.*
> *Her leaders are only human*
> *and their efforts will be for nothing*
> *unless you are their guide.*
> *Her institutions and agencies*
> *are choked with their structure and form*
> *unless you are their Lord.*

Come with your power to all the various ways
by which we strive to improve our human condition,
to our hospitals, our welfare departments,
our schools, our governments.
Make us honest and perceptive

and determined to serve with efficiency and zeal.
Look upon all of our human endeavors,
and give us the grace to be more understanding,
one of another,
and more willing to go to each other's help.
> *Sustain our faith in you and in your son, Jesus.*
> *Remind us, when we pity our lot,*
> *that he suffered unjustly,*
> *and died for what seemed to be no clear reason.*
> *Yet at the last he made defeat into victory,*
> *death into life.*
> *Let us see life,*
> *O God,*
> *through the same Jesus Christ, your son, our Lord,*
> *who lives and rules with you and the Spirit,*
> *one God forever. Amen.*

57 A Time of Great Joy

Eternal God,
your goodness is greater than anything we could imagine,
and we rejoice because of your love.
We have new life from you
in the gift of Jesus Christ.
We have a common concern and a deep affection,
one for another.
We have repeated reasons for believing in you
and in your gracious presence in our lives.
> *Help us,*
> *O God,*
> *that as we live we may be thankful,*
> *not only for life,*
> *but for its every part,*
> *for all the seasons with their various gifts,*
> *for all who live,*
> *for our nourishment and our shelter.*

Come,
dear Lord,
to all men everywhere
in accordance with what may happen to be their needs.
Make us, each one,
more quick to speak in charity
than in anger with our brother,
and give us the desire to reach to one another in love.

*Cut into the prejudice and hardness of heart
that prevents the exchange of understanding and opinion.
Overthrow tyranny
wherever it may stifle the human spirit,
and as men are denied their freedom
because of fear or ignorance or the misuse of power,
break through
with new manifestations of your truth
made alive in your people.*
Give your guidance to our nation
and to all in positions of authority.
End the long winter of conflict on the earth
with peace that is just and lasting.
Speak to any discontent that may plague us,
so that our unrest may find creative channels
and our grievances appropriate solutions.
*Help the church,
O God,
and her institutions and agencies.
Be with this congregation.
Overcome our indifference and our apathy,
and remind us of the joy that is at the heart of our faith.
Make us more fully aware
of what you intend for your people.
Watch over those of our number who are far distant,
and any who are distressed or discouraged,
and to all bring your love,
through Jesus Christ, your son, our Lord,
who lives and rules with you and the Spirit,
one God forever. Amen.*

58   Peace

Hear us, Lord.
> *Hear us, Lord.*

That we may come to know your love,
> *hear us, Lord.*

That we may draw closer, one to another,
> *hear us, Lord.*

That we may reach out, one to another,
> *hear us, Lord.*

That we may forgive,
> *hear us, Lord.*

That we may be forgiven,
> *hear us, Lord.*

That we may open our minds,
> *hear us, Lord.*

That we may see others as they are,
> *hear us, Lord.*

That we may love others as they are,
> *hear us, Lord.*

That we may serve others as they are,
> *hear us, Lord.*

Come to the difficult places of life,
> *hear us, Lord.*

Come to the battlefields of the world,
> *hear us, Lord.*

Come to the halls of government,
> *hear us, Lord.*

Come to the armories and the munition factories,
> *hear us, Lord.*

Come to the hospitals and the morgues,
> *hear us, Lord.*

Stop the selfish manipulations of selfish men,
> *hear us, Lord.*

Stop the hatred and the lack of trust,
> *hear us, Lord.*

Stop the cruelty and the intolerance and the injustice,
> *hear us, Lord.*

Stop the killing,
> *hear us, Lord.*

Show us how to live in peace,
> *hear us, Lord.*

Show us how to love our neighbors,
> *hear us, Lord.*

Show us how to work for freedom,
> *hear us, Lord.*

Make us into agents of your will,
> *hear us, Lord.*

Make us brave enough to stand for peace,
> *hear us, Lord.*

Make us wise enough to see what leads to peace,
> *hear us, Lord.*

Give peace, Lord.
> *Give peace. Amen.*

VII

A Set of Affirmations and Petitions for Use in Ecumenical Gatherings

Leader: We are the people of God,
and we are one in Christ.

People: We are one in Christ.

Leader: We are in a new age,
and our unity is made more clear,
an indication of our Lord's intention
that all be one in him.

People: We are one in Christ.

Leader: Challenged by our world,
and alive within it,
we rejoice to discover our common concerns,
and are heartened by our common devotion.

People: We are one in Christ.

Leader: Yet it is not that our oneness comes
only as we renounce our inheritance.
It is rather that we come, as the Magi,
each with his gift to the Lord
whose body is the church,
each with his saints.

*One of the
Reformed tradition:*
We give Calvin, and Knox, and Wesley.
We give order, and simplicity, and justice.

People: And we are grateful for the gift.

One of the
Baptist tradition:
      We give Williams, and Moody, and Graham.
      We give emotion, and fervor, and freedom.

People: And we are grateful for the gift.

One of the
Lutheran tradition:
      We give Luther, and Bach, and Bonhoeffer.
      We give theology, and music, and piety.

People: And we are grateful for the gift.

One of the
Roman Catholic tradition:
      We give Augustine, and Aquinas, and John XXIII.
      We give structure, and heritage, and renewal.

People: And we are grateful for the gift.

Leader: For all the kinds of Christians,
      we are grateful,
      acknowledging the Spirit's work in our distinctions,
      and praying for the grace to perceive
      the divisiveness that pride creates.
      In that we are separated brethren
      by reason of our own fault,
      perpetuating the sins of the centuries,

People: forgive us, dear Lord.

Leader: Nor is it only as members of different denominations
that we are one in Christ.
It is also as God's people
seeking his service
that we give to one another our gifts.

A physician:
I give healing, and relief from pain.

A social worker:
I give counsel,
and support for the overburdened and bewildered.

A legislator:
I give law and order,
the governing of society
for the good of all by the will of all.

A secretary:
I give my typing, and filing,
and telephoning, and scheduling.

A merchant:
I give the stuff of life,
food and clothing and all things needful.

Leader: All give as they can
with their skills and their interests,
artists and musicians,
teachers and students,
craftsmen and laborers.

          In our common devotion
          to the needs of our world,

People: we are one in Christ.

Leader: And from our places of life
          we come with our gifts,
             to enrich and strengthen and uphold each other.

One from a suburb:
          We give stability,
          and the ideals of home and family.

One from a young adult area:
          We give color, and ingenuity, and youth.

One from the center city:
          We give the way of the future,
          the values of the world men make.

One from the inner city:
          And we give you your greatest need!

Leader: From our places of life we come with our gifts,
          with our talents and our vocations,
          as we are in the Lord.
          And as we are, now, we pray.
          For this, our oneness in Christ,

People: Lord, we thank you.

*One of the
Reformed tradition:*
>For the hope of the city of God,

People: Lord, we thank you.

*One of the
Baptist tradition:*
>For the determination to be found
>as free men before you,

People: Lord, we thank you.

*One of the
Lutheran tradition:*
>For faith that trusts in you alone,

People: Lord, we thank you.

*One of the
Roman Catholic tradition:*
>For the continuing renewal of your church,

People: Lord, we thank you.

A physician:
>Guide the learning of men,
>that we may increasingly overcome
>human disease and affliction.

People: We ask you to hear us, good Lord.

A social worker:
>Help us to discover the causes of poverty
>and ignorance and social disorder,
>that men everywhere may live in peace and plenty.

People: We ask you to hear us, good Lord.

A legislator:
>Be with the mayor of this city,
>the governor of this state,
>the president of this nation,
>and all rulers everywhere,
>that they may govern with justice and wisdom.

People: We ask you to hear us, good Lord.

A secretary:
>Give us a sense of your purpose in what we do,
>that each may in his way
>be of service to our society.

People: We ask you to hear us, good Lord.

A merchant:
>Reach to the needs of all
>with the materials of life,
>that none within our care
>might go hungry or naked or homeless.

People: We ask you to hear us, good Lord.

One from a suburb:
> Where we have isolated ourselves
> from the problems of the city
> while gaining out of it our livelihood,

People: Lord, have mercy upon us.

One from a young adult area:
> Where we have rejected the young,
> and the creative, and the different,

People: Lord, have mercy upon us.

One from the center city:
> Where we have sought to rise above the noisy clangor,
> and so have eluded the sight of human need,

People: Lord, have mercy upon us.

One from the inner city:
> And where we have failed,
> because we have run away,
> and because we have not cared enough,
> and because we have little faith,

People: Lord, have mercy upon us.

Leader: Christ, have mercy upon us.

People: Lord, have mercy upon us.

All: Amen.

VIII

Intercessions

Let us pray for the whole people of God in Christ Jesus and for all men according to their needs.

For the People of God

Father, we are your people, called together in your name. Make us one in spirit and purpose, and move in us to all the world with your love.
Lord, in your mercy,
> *hear our prayer.*

For Evangelism

So many do not know you, and too often it is because they cannot see you in us. Help us come alive with concern for your people, that men may come to faith in you and in your son, Jesus Christ.
Lord, in your mercy,
> *hear our prayer.*

For the Ministry

Strengthen our understanding that we have all been called to do your will in the world, and help those whom we elect to be our pastors that they may enable us and uphold us and work with us in the fulfillment of our common ministry.
Lord, in your mercy,
> *hear our prayer.*

For Seminaries

Where men and women gather to study your word and will, come with power and understanding, that new life

may enter your church as new servants of her people complete their preparations for ministry.
Lord, in your mercy,
> *hear our prayer.*

For Church Meetings

Father, (name of group) meets (time of meeting) . Come with your Spirit to this assembly, and cause its actions to be worthy reflections of your concern for our world.
Lord, in your mercy,
> *hear our prayer.*

For World Missions

Look upon our efforts throughout the world to minister to human need. Help us as we seek to help others through education and the relief of hunger, nakedness, homelessness, and disease. Counsel us as we seek to tell people about you and your love, that your word may be apparent in our deeds and our lives.
Lord, in your mercy,
> *hear our prayer.*

For the Persecuted

Your people in some places must suffer greatly because of their faith in you. Give them courage to remain faithful, the assurance of our concern for them, and relief from the oppression.
Lord, in your mercy,
> *hear our prayer.*

For Dialogue

> Give us a willingness to listen to one another, and even to those with whom we have sharp disagreements, lest in blind obedience to what we call the truth we do not hear your word as you elect to speak it through the words of others.
> Lord, in your mercy,
>> *hear our prayer.*

For the Sick

> Be with your servants, (name), who are ill, and strengthen them with your grace. Attend those who minister to them, their physicians and nurses, and give them insight and guidance. By your will give healing to the sick, and peace.
> Lord, in your mercy,
>> *hear our prayer.*

For the Seriously Injured

> Look upon your servant, (name), who is gravely injured. Ease *his* pain, and hasten the healing of *his* body, and keep *him* in your care.
> Lord, in your mercy,
>> *hear our prayer.*

For the Dying

> Father, your servant, (name), is dying. You have given *him* life, and redeemed *him* by the death of your son, Jesus Christ, and you have lived in *him* through

your Holy Spirit. Now receive *him* unto yourself, and may *his* rest be this day in paradise.
Lord, in your mercy,
> *hear our prayer.*

For the Sorrowing
Father, look upon the family and friends of ___(name)___. Comfort them in this time of loss with the assurance of your love and the promise of eternal life.
Lord, in your mercy,
> *hear our prayer.*

For the New Year
Be our leader and our guide through the year to come, O God. Help us to grow in our understanding of you and of one another. Protect us from harm, and keep us faithful, and grant us joy.
Lord, in your mercy,
> *hear our prayer.*

For the Fruits of the Earth in Their Season
Father, we are grateful for this fair earth and its riches. Be with those who till its soil and mine its wealth and timber its forests, that we may continue to share the bounty of this earth so that each may have enough for his need.
Lord, in your mercy,
> *hear our prayer.*

For Elections

We are about to select those who will be our leaders. Give us the good sense to vote wisely, so that we will choose those most qualified to rule us.
Lord, in your mercy,
> *hear our prayer.*

For the Nation

Let your favor rest upon us as a nation, not that we may be more blessed than the other nations of this earth, but rather that we may see ourselves as a people brought together for our common good and for the welfare of other people in other lands.
Lord, in your mercy,
> *hear our prayer.*

For Our Leaders

Look upon the president of this nation, (name) , the governor of this state, (name) , and the mayor of this city, (name) . Help them to be wise, and just, and compassionate as they fulfill their responsibilities.
Lord, in your mercy,
> *hear our prayer.*

For Those in the Armed Forces

Bless those who serve their country in the armed forces. Direct them with your truth as they do their difficult work, and be their companion when they must engage

in battle. Bless also our enemies, and hasten the day when men shall lay down their arms forever.
Lord, in your mercy,
> *hear our prayer.*

For Social Justice
Many of your children are denied opportunity because of their race or nationality or creed. Strike down those who conspire to prevent equality for all people, and open closed doors, and bring freedom.
Lord, in your mercy,
> *hear our prayer.*

For the Community
Help us to see ourselves as a part of a larger community, and encourage us to find ways in which we can be the vehicles of your love reaching out to those who need you here where we endeavor to minister in your name.
Lord, in your mercy,
> *hear our prayer.*

For Brotherhood
We are so often tempted to think of ourselves as different from others. Teach us to think of ourselves as identical to others, created equal by your love, of equal value in your sight. Let us then live as brothers, children of one father.
Lord, in your mercy,
> *hear our prayer.*

For Peace

Father, you know the futility of our wars. Bring us to our senses, that throughout all the world men may beat their swords into plows and learn to live in love, that the dread sounds of battle may never again come with death and destruction upon the land.
Lord, in your mercy,
> *hear our prayer.*

For the Poor

Behold those who struggle to stay alive, who have not enough of the necessities of life, who despair for their future because of their poverty and their need, and help us to help them.
Lord, in your mercy,
> *hear our prayer.*

For the Imprisoned

Many of your children are imprisoned, and often they are so denied human dignity that their confinement is only a punishment and not a means of rehabilitation. Prevent that from happening, and enlighten correction officers and others who are involved in this work, that those imprisoned may be returned to useful and responsible lives within society.
Lord, in your mercy,
> *hear our prayer.*

For the Aged

Look upon the elderly, dear God. Give them strength for the infirmities of age, companions for their lonely hours, and a sense of purpose and meaning for their lives.
Lord, in your mercy,
hear our prayer.

For Industrial Peace

Be a mediating force between labor and management, and encourage both to consider the special problems of the other, so that their negotiations may be conducted in an atmosphere of mutual understanding and result in agreements that are of mutual benefit.
Lord, in your mercy,
hear our prayer.

For the Unemployed

Some of your people would work if they could, but circumstances have denied them employment. Give them patience under this adversity, and direct them to new possibilities for their vocation, and help us find the ways we can help them.
Lord, in your mercy,
hear our prayer.

For Contending with the Perils of Abundance

We are rich while so many are poor. We have more than enough for our needs while so many struggle to stay alive. Prevent us from measuring the quality of life by the quantity of our possessions, and help us to keep our perspective, lest in gaining this whole world we lose your love.
Lord, in your mercy,
hear our prayer.

For Those Who Travel

Be with those who travel by land or sea or air. Protect them against harm, and grant them a safe return to their homes and loved ones.
Lord, in your mercy,
hear our prayer.

For Students

Some of our number are students, preparing themselves for their work in life. Instruct them in your truth, that they may see their lives as intended for the service of your world and your people.
Lord, in your mercy,
hear our prayer.

For Those About to be Married

We pray for (name) and (name), who are to come together as man and wife (time). Deepen

their love for one another, and give their marriage your blessing.
Lord, in your mercy,
> *hear our prayer.*

For the Children
Look upon the young, and surround them with those who care about them, so that they may learn about you and your love for them and grow up to serve you and others with joy and devotion.
Lord, in your mercy,
> *hear our prayer.*

For a Wedding Anniversary
We are grateful for the (number) anniversary of the wedding of (names) , and we praise you for these years of love and service.
Lord, in your mercy,
> *hear our prayer.*

For Family Life
Uphold us in our families, dear father. Keep us committed to one another, and in love with one another, and delighted by each other, so that all of us in our homes, mothers and fathers and children, may live in peace and joy, to the service of others and in faith toward you.
Lord, in your mercy,
> *hear our prayer.*

For Christians and Jews

Forgive us for the hostility that continues to exist, father, between Christians and Jews. We share a common heritage in your revealed word. Let that word lead to the healing of wounds and the deepening of understanding, that in the name of the Jew whom Christians call their savior we may find new ways of building the kingdom together.

Lord, in your mercy,

hear our prayer.

For Those Who Have Just Been Baptized

We rejoice in the baptism of (names) , father. Give *him* your presence all *his* life, and as *he* has been baptized into our body, the church, give us new resolve to minister to *him* and to all your children.

Lord, in your mercy,

hear our prayer.

For Those Who Have Just Been Married

Your servants, (name) and (name) were joined in marriage (time) . Cause their union to be a blessing to them and to others, deepen their affection to each other and their desire to serve each other, and help them to consider you as the Lord of their home and lives.

Lord, in your mercy,

hear our prayer.

For the Memory of the Dead in Christ

(On the anniversary of the death of members of the congregation, let their names be read together with the use of the following intercession.)

>We call to mind, father, the following members of our congregation who entered into life with you forever on this day in past years:
>(names) (years)
>
>Hallow their memory among us, and as in dying, they live, grant us to live in faith and love, and, at the end of our years in this world, to be received into your eternal home.
>Lord, in your mercy,
>>*hear our prayer.*

Into your hands, father, we commend all for whom we pray, trusting in your mercy, through your son, Jesus Christ our Lord. Amen.

IX

Dialogue Prayers

59 Vocations

(As possible, let the various petitions be read by people who are engaged in the vocations named.)

Leader: From the many places of our lives,
O Lord,
we come to you.
See us in our need for your love,
and sustain us as we serve you and our world
through our work and calling.

Business: Uphold your people who serve
through the conduct of their businesses.

Transportation: Uphold your people who serve
by maintaining the arteries of transportation.

Teaching: Uphold your people who serve
as teachers and counselors of the young.

Farming: Uphold your people who serve
by the cultivation of the earth.

Military service: Uphold your people who serve
through the armed forces of our nation.

Healing arts: Uphold your people who serve
by ministering to the afflictions of others.

Construction: Uphold your people who serve
as the builders of our roads
and our homes and our structures.

Performing arts: Uphold your people who serve
through their music and drama and dance.

Ministry: Uphold your people who serve
by the preaching of your word
and the administration of the sacraments.

Food services: Uphold your people who serve
by meeting our needs for food and drink.

Homemaking: Uphold your people who serve
as the homemakers within our families.

Communications: Uphold your people who serve
through the many different forms
of communication.

Data processing: Uphold your people who serve
by their involvement in data processing
procedures

Creative arts: Uphold your people who serve
with their painting and sculpture
and photography and music.

Engineering: Uphold your people who serve
through the careful execution of plans
and the design of the things we need.

Law: Uphold your people who serve
as our advisors and advocates within the law.

Factory workers: Uphold your people who serve
by producing the things we need
in our factories.

Government: Uphold your people who serve
through their functions as government workers.

Office personnel: Uphold your people who serve
as secretaries and clerks
and bookkeepers and receptionists.

Here may be inserted similar petitions
for any other vocations not named

Leader: Look also,
dear God,
upon your people who find themselves
without calling or purpose.
Reach to them with your love,
and give them meaning and direction.
Yet caution us,

lest in our pride of our calling
and our zeal for our work
we forget our humanity or our faith.
Move us to the use of our talents
for the needs of your people,
and help us live as did your son,
the carpenter Jesus Christ.
We pray in his name. Amen.

60 Youth

Leader: Eternal father,
we know that in your sight
our differences disappear.
All of us are your children,
and your concern is no less
for one of us than for another.

A young person: We are the ones who set up the differences.
We create countless distinctions
based on the accidents of our birth.
We erect walls between the rich and the poor,
the black and the white,
the young and the old.

An adult: Forgive us, Lord.
Forgive us for our conceit and our envy.
Forgive us for treating each other as things.
Forgive us for thinking that everyone else
ought to be like us.

Leader: See us where we contend with others
because they are younger or older.
Touch the wounds we have opened
by our stubborness and pride,
and bring us healing.

A young person: Help us come to a new awareness
of our heritage and tradition.
Give us the patience to learn,
and an appreciation of those who teach.

An adult: Help us come to a new awareness
of our future and our hope.
Prevent us from having closed minds.
Challenge us to learn to live with change.

Leader: Make us ministers of your love.
As Christ came to seek and to serve,
guide us into those places of our lives
where we can live in imitation of him.

A young person: Direct us to those who need us,
the infirm, the aged, the helpless.
Correct us when we think there's nothing we can do.

An adult: Arouse our anger over the waste of the earth
by pollution and affluence and war.
Give us the courage to act
upon our convictions
in ways that will have their effect.

Leader: And as any of our fellowship are in need,
reach to them and love them, father,
even as your love came to all our world
through Jesus Christ, your son, our Lord,
who lives and rules with you and the Spirit,
one God forever. Amen.

61   Various Ages

Leader: We come from the various ages of our lives, father,
offering what we are
and asking that your love
will continue,
age after age,
year after year.

A child: Be with your people who are children.
Help their teachers and parents.
Keep them from harm and danger.
Make them strong, and wise, and happy.

An elderly person: Be with your people who are old.
Give them patience for their infirmities,
and companions for their lonely hours.
Give them new evidence of your love,
and teach them to trust you
above all others.

A young person: Be with your people who are young.
Encourage their enthusiasm,
resolve their doubts and anxieties,
and lengthen their perspectives.

A middle-aged person: Be with your people who are middle-aged.
Help them to deal with their fears

for themselves and their families.
Preserve them from boredom
and selfishness and indulgence
and other bad fruits
of our affluent society.

Leader: See us in our stages in life,
father,
and come to us in our needs.
Show us how we need each other,
and suggest the ways in which we can
come together.

A child: Give those of us who are children
the love of those who might be
our grandparents.
We need the time they can give to us,
and their love.

An elderly person: Give those of us who are old
young children whom we might spoil
with our love.
We need their smiles and joy,
their innocent view of life.

A young person: Give those of us who are young
the friendship of those who might be
our parents.
We need their interest in our lives,
their counsel and advice.

A middle-aged person: Give those of us who are middle-aged
the young whom we might see
as if seeing ourselves.
We need their carefree confidence,
their newer ways of thinking and doing.

Leader: Our times are in your hands,
father,
and a thousand years in your sight
are like a day.
You know that the youngest among us
will become the oldest,
that even the oldest is but a child
before you.
Help us to see what we need from
one another,
and how we can help one another,
as did Jesus Christ, your son, our Lord,
who lives and rules with you
and the Spirit,
one God forever. Amen.

62   Men and Women

Leader: Father,
you have made us male and female,
ordained that our very life
come from the union of the sexes,
fashioned our world in such a way
that this distinction
is within its very structure.
For what we are,

       we give you thanks.

A woman: For tenderness and gentleness and pity,
for the love of beauty
and order and tranquility,
for the instinct to give shelter
and nourish and enfold,
for all that is of woman,

       we give you thanks.

A man: For decisiveness and action and strength,
for the love of precision
and accomplishment and endeavor,
for the instinct to protect
and lead and determine,
for all that is of man,

       we give you thanks.

A woman: And yet,
Lord,
women can also be strong.
Why must we be treated as if we were weak
and incompetent and unworthy?

A man: And,
Lord,
men can also love beauty.
Why must we be treated as if we were
insensitive and unfeeling?

Leader: Look to our needs to be human.
Help us to see ourselves as complete persons,
and give us the sense to allow others
to be themselves.

A woman: Set women free
from the expectations of others
and the chains of tradition
and the pressures of society.

A man: Set men free
from their need to dominate
and their fear of change
and their pride.

A woman: Yet let us be completely human
by allowing us to be sexually complete.
Help women to continue to cherish

| | womanly things,
homes and families,
recipes and fashions. |
| --- | --- |
| *A man:* | And help men to continue to be men,
workers with their hands and minds,
mechanics and farmers and outdoorsmen,
concerned for athletics
and tools and motors. |
| *Leader:* | So may it be,
father,
that as we are we praise you
by coming together in the order of your creation,
each adding our sexuality
and our being as humans
created by you for your world.
Increase our respect and regard
one for another,
and teach us to gain from each other
that our lives may be fulfilled.
We pray in the name of Jesus. Amen. |

63   Various Congregational Concerns

Members of the congregation must elect their participation in this prayer. Possibly an individual would feel that he could participate in every section, but it will be more effective if he selects only one statement of greatest interest, and participates in reading only one of the three paragraphs of prayer with which this dialogue concludes.

A representative layman
We are come together, one with another, from many places, from many homes, from many walks in life;

Pastor
And it is in the name of God that we are here assembled, our father in that he created us, our Lord in that he saved us, our strength in that he moves in and through us;

The lay president of the congregation
And it is as the church of Jesus Christ that we are here, the unique structure in this world that endeavors to do the work of God in mercy and in love.

A representative layman
We have our several concerns as God's family, our convictions about the needs of our present day. As his grace comes alive in us and in others we can anticipate its good effect, the renewal he would bring to us and to others.

Those mostly concerned for parish education
God's word would flower as learning became the way of our lives, as in excitement we would grow in our understanding of our world and of one another and of the love of God.

Those mostly concerned for tithes and offerings
All that we have and are would be judged as belonging to all the world and to God. In joy we would live responsibly and responsively for our neighbor's good.

Those mostly concerned for higher education
Our schools would fashion the men and women of tomorrow in lives of noble virtue, and those institutions which are of the church would reach new excellence in their appointed work, while those that are of the larger community would have increasing numbers within them who would speak with conviction in the name of God.

Those mostly concerned for world missions
The challenges of our age would be met with compassion and humility, the gospel proclaimed in its simple truth and not as an extension of our culture, the love of Christ made known in acts of love, without price or demand.

Those mostly concerned for evangelism
Men in this day would hear the word in their words, cutting to their nature and to their condition, clear in its truth, convincing in its power, able to give peace and make peace. They would see the word in deeds.

Those mostly concerned for social ministry
The word made alive in our society would fashion a new condition for men, destroying the old hatreds and the ancient mistakes, causing concern to be the way of our life and justice to be the right of all.

A representative layman
Could all of this come to be? Could the word come that much alive in us, where we are and as we are?

The lay president of the congregation
To this we address ourselves as a people, else all we do is but emptiness and idle work.

Pastor
That the word might come alive in us, let us pray.
Eternal God, we are your servants, come to this place from our many places, one as we are united in the church of Jesus Christ, yet many and diverse as we bring to this assembly our several interests and desires. With these, our diversities, that we might be one, we pray:

Those mostly concerned for the transformation of individuals
Enable by your Spirit, O God, all who minister in the name of Jesus Christ, that men may come to believe in him and accept his love, that their lives may be renewed and reborn. Create a new measure of faith and hope, that the way of Christ may be the way of all men everywhere, to the increase of his kingdom among us.

Those mostly concerned for the transformation of society
Stir our complacency, O God, by which we have ignored your clear will for our land, and come with your cleansing power into the structures of our society, that inequities and corruption and oppression may cease, and men may live in peace and dignity, one with another and for the common good.

Those mostly concerned for reconciliation
Give to us a vision of our role for these times, dear God, that will set us to the healing of wounds and the breaking down of barriers. Cause us to be the makers of peace, and give us the courage so to live with others that your love in us will be as salt and yeast and light.

Pastor
And go with us into the world, father, that men may know you in knowing us, even as we see your love in Jesus Christ, who lives and rules with you and the Spirit, one God forever. Amen.